ACADEMIC TRIUMPHS

The Journey To Excellence

DR. SWATI MISHRA

TRUE SIGN
PUBLISHING HOUSE

Published by True Sign Publishing House
Address: SY. No. 21/2 & 21/3, Sonnenahalli,
Krishnarajapura, Bengaluru,
Karnataka - 560049 India
E-mail: truesignbooks@gmail.com
Website: www.truesign.in

Academic Triumphs: The Journey To Excellence

Author: Dr. Swati Mishra

ISBN: 978-93-5904-442-2

First Edition: 2023

PREFACE

The educational quality is the key to the development of any country, students receive better education and perfect approach for knowledge, and they achieve higher goals thus giving their best for the development of society. Education is the broadest area considered for the development of human resources. It is the process of acquiring the mental abilities and thus enhancing the potential of an individual.

Academic performance is a wider term of educational growth. It is a unique, prime responsibility of an educational institution established by a society to promote a wholesome academic growth and development of the individual. Academic performance implies the learning performance of students in their institution. It is considered as a key to judge an "individual's potential and capacity." The academic performance largely depends on parenting practices, intelligence, study habits, motivation, level of aspiration, family and school environment, etc. In this connection it was thought appropriate that some personality factors, morningness-eveningnesss preference affect the academic performance of the engineering students. This important aspect has not been given due attention by the researchers, especially in Chhattisgarh state, it has been almost neglected. Therefore, the present study was undertaken with a view to examine the role of different personality factors namely, neuroticism, extraversion, openness, agreeableness and conscientiousness, morningness-eveningness preference and gender on academic performance of the technical students.

I express my heartiest sentiments and special thanks to my parents whose blessings and inspiration were greatly instrumental in accomplishing this work. My brother, husband and all my friends whose continuous support has made this work possible.

THANK YOU

DR. SWATI MISHRA

CONTENTS

Chapter One

DIVING INTO THE REALM OF EDUCATIONAL PERFORMANCE

The development of any nation depends upon the progress of their agricultural, industrial, human resources, health and educational services. Though, development of human resources seems to be rudimentary for all other growths. With developed human resources, a nation can attain excellence in every area. Education is a comprehensive and an important area in the human development. Education is either formal or informal and is an important contributor of individual personality. It is the process of acquiring the mental abilities and potential of the human. So to prepare that individual to be successful in a specific society and culture, it begins at birth and carries on throughout life. Education shapes the personality as desired by the individual and society. The educational system evaluated by the society to develop its future citizens, who in turn will become the right way of life **(Kumar, 2013)**. Education is the most important part of the students' development, every person should have the opportunity to achieve his or her academic potential **(Karande & Kulkarni, 2005)**.

The quality of education is the key to the development of any country, although the student's receive better education and perfect approach for knowledge they achieve higher and also they give their best to the development of the society. Good quality academic performance helps to acquire self-esteem, self-respect and assurance and helps the individual to make a spot for himself in the competition ridden society. Many factors largely affect the educational system and its achievement and they have their relative effect on society. The several intentions of an individual's capacity of understanding the world around them **(Jain & Helode, 1989)**. Achievement can be stated as performing in terms of standard of excellence or simply as a desire to be successful. Academic performance is a fundamental goal in the education area. Academic performance is a component of the wider term of educational growth. It is a unique, prime responsibility of an educational institution established by a society to promote a wholesome academic growth and development of the individuals. Academic performance means the student's success in their academic subjects in the context of their knowledge or capability in school or college tasks, it is measured by the standardized tests and expressed in grades based on the student's overall performance. Academic performance is directly related to a student's growth and development of knowledge in an educational situation where the teaching-learning process takes place **(Pandey, 2008)**. Academic performance is frequently defined in terms of examination performance **(Cambridge University Reporter, 2003).** According to **Steinberger (1993)** "academic performance encompasses the student's ability and performance, it is multi-dimensional, it is intricately related to human growth and emotional, cognitive, social and physical development, it reflects the whole child; it is not related to a particular instance, but occurs across time and levels, through a student's life in community schools and on to post secondary years and working life". **Varghese (2005)** stated that the academic performance implies the learning performance of students in their institution. It is considered as a key to judge an individual's potential and capacity. In other words, academic performance may be defined as competence, students actually show in their subjects in which they have received instruction **(Singh, 2012).**

Many educational institutions's stated that the success is evaluated by academic performance and the student's meets standard institution itself. Students' doing well in their institution captures the attention of parents, teacher and their institute. Academic performance affects many aspects of psychology like attitude, intelligence, ability, thinking style, creativity, aptitude, personality, etc. It's also affected by the factor of biological and environmental. Educational performance is a very enormous term which includes a lot of factors that contributes to the satisfaction, intelligence, interest, mental and physical health, personality, intelligence, ability, etc.

Importance of Academic Performance

Our society is changing everyday and also demands high achievers. The success is considered as the highest expectation to provide challenges and encouragement essential to press on the student's highest performance and everyone is encouraged to succeed and considered essential role of the member of society **(Ozturk & Debelak, 2005).**

Academic performance has a comprehensive importance in personal life. It can be identified as the excelling of a student in academics, by manner of attaining high-quality levels, which will ensure the way to a successful career in future life. The principal aim of assessing academic performance is to ascertain the points to which academic objectives of an institutional system or something to do or achieve at school, college or university in class, research lab and library or field study. It is the outcome of education, the extent to which student's, teachers or institution has achieved their educational goals. It may be defined as the performance of the study at the institute. Students gain knowledge and develop skills in the institutional environment and become competent in the subjects which they study during an academic session. Academic brilliance ensures the social maturation of not just the person, but also the refinement with which he/she is very much concerned. Students assume a system of schooling which plays a significant function in academic progress, as considerably as the teaching patterns of the institute, there are other dimensions which enable successful academic achievement among pupils. A quick to respond institute climate, which involves parents and caretakers in the process of education, has a positive effect on the educational as well as the social development of the pupil. Thus, we can conclude that academic performance aim is to take care of a student and facilitate his/her professional, community and personal development, which would be beneficial to the integral residential district and cannot be achieved, only the educational institutions or educators, but the parents have a decisive part in assisting their pupils reach their goal or success. The importance of academic performance can be evaluated when we realize a fuller and a happier life, which we wish for every scholar would be impossible unless he has reached a high grade of proficiency in his studies. Academic performance to a great extent predicts the future of student, also, it is the singular obligation of all educational institutions set up by society to push the whole scholastic development of the pupils. The importance of academic performance can be judged when we realize a fuller and a happier life, which we wish for every student, would be impossible unless he has attained a high degree of proficiency in his subjects. Academic performance to a great extent predicts the future of students, also, it is the unique responsibility of all educational institutions established by society to promote the whole scholastic development of the students.

Factors affecting Academic Performance

Academic performance is the most important area of a student's life. It's a very essential topic for educational and psychological inquiry. Various researches have been taken to convey in the image of various genes that influence academic performance. Many factors influence the academic performance of students, including admission points, socio-economic status, family and school background and some personal factors i.e., physical and mental status. In the present circumstance, there are numerous studies on correlates of academic performance so it is very complicated to classify them. However, the factors affecting academic performance can be grouped into some categories, i.e., (1). Institutional factors which include teacher-student relationship, school/college environment, teaching style, curricular activities, etc. (2). Family factors which include family environment, socio-economic status, parent involvement, parental education, etc. (3). Personal factors which include interest, intelligence, study habit, aptitude, motivation, creativity, aspiration level and physical and mental health, etc.

Institutional Factors

The institutional factors are most likely to be a responsible factor for academic performance. Most researches helped in the identification of some variables and institutional factors associated with a student's performance.

Institutions influence the learning in the sense of teaching process, learning assessment procedures, etc. affects the academic performance **(Sentamu, 2003)**. The environment of the institute has a significant impact on the students performance **(Maehr & Midgley, 1996)**. **Renchler (1992)** suggested that effective climate of school enhances the academic performance. **Fraser (1994)** also suggested that psychological and sociological circumstances are the determinants of academic performance. School management reports significant effect on academic performance **(Taj, 1999; Varghese, 1995).**

Numerous studies demonstrate that atmosphere of institution and climate influence the academic performance such as **(Ahluwalia, 1990; Ganihar & Shaik, 2004; Marchant, Paulson & Rothlissberg, 2001; Panda, Sahoo & Sahoo, 1995; Reddy, 1994; Sananda Raj & Sreethi, 2000; Salili & Lai, 2003)**. In the classroom, students do most of the learning task, so the classroom environment facilitates students' performance **(Fisher, 1992; Fraser & Walberg, 1991). Cheng (1994)** found the classroom environment to affect students learning attitude and its influence on their performance. **Adetoro (2001); Ozerk (2001)** suggested that the small size of the class provides condition to better academic performance. **Kwesige (2002)** found that school facilities and quality of school influence the academic performance.

The types of institution also affect the learning outcomes **(Considine & Zappala, 2002)**. Several studies indicated such as **Felder, Dietz, Mohr and Ward (1994); Kolcic (2006)** school background affects the student performance and the students performed better in urban areas than in the rural areas. **Ross and Berthelot (2001); Considine and Zappala (2002)** indicated that the urban school students performed better than the rural school students.

The teaching style is a significant predictor of academic performance **(Govinda & Varghese, 1993; Merchant, Paulson & Rothlisberg, 2001)**. The teacher's behaviour and effectiveness, influence academic performance **(Reynolds, 2002; Wood, Murdock & Cronin, 2002). Alfassi, (2003); Luyben, Hipworth and Pappas (2003)** reported that the instructional programs show significant impact on academic performance.

The teacher-student relationship plays a more important role in student performance **(Burke, 1996; Jacobson, 2000; Liu, 1997; Steete, 1992). Hunt (2003)** revealed that teacher-student interaction is a critical variable in the educational destiny of students and this interaction contributes to better academic performance **(Ozerk, 2001; Suneetha & Mayuri, 2000).** Studies have been concluded that teacher-student relations are related to the higher degree of academic performance **(Niebuhr & Niebuhr, 1999).**

The involvement in extra-curricular activities and efficient learning good for personal development helps to make better academic performance **(Camp, 1990; Cairns & Farmer, 2003; De Moulin, 2002; Finn & Rock, 1997; Gifford & Dean, 1990; Marsh, 1992)**. Students' extra-curricular activities improve the academic performance **(Broh, 2002). Gerber (1996)** reported that type of extra activities promote greater academic performance.

Family Factors

The family structure plays an important role in influencing the child's whole personality and their performance in society. The educational performance, highly affected by the family factors, i.e. family background, family structure, parental education, parenting style and parental occupation and incomes are associated with academic performance **(Jacob & Harvey, 2005).** The high status of the family provides better psychological support of their children and help with their academic performance **(Williams, Lony, Carpenter & Hayden, 1993)**. Parental education has influenced the academic performance of students. Educated parents' child show better academic performance **(Borbora, 2001). Sentamu (2003)** revealed that illiterate parents' child showed lower levels of academic success. Social class of parents has significant effects on students' performance **(Taj, 1999; Vanlaar & Sidarius, 2001). Escarce (2003)** suggested that the availability of educational opportunities affected the student's performance and support the concepts of students by family, such as, economic circumstances are correlated with academic performance.

Socio-economic status is the most important determinant of academic performance **(McMillan & Western, 2000; Jeynes, 2002). Considine and Zappala (2002); Graetz (1995)** found that the influence of social and economic status was a disadvantage in academic performance. **Williams, Long, Carpenter and Hayden (1993)** suggested that higher level of family status help with performance and provides better psychological support, economic conditions are also associated with academic performance **(Okpala, Okpala & Smith, 2001)**. Higher socio-economic status has shown a higher degree of academic talent **(Sinha,**

1992). Dills (2006) found higher economic status students perform better. **Newcomb, Abbott, Catalano and Hawkins (2002)** revealed that most of the failure is related to family socio-economic status.

Parental involvement also influences the students' academic outcomes **(Badhri, 1991; Marchant, Paulson & Rothlisberg, 2001; Taj, 1999). Bagenschneider (1997)** reported that the parental involvement is a potential predictor of students' success which strongly affected students' performance **(Van Voorhis, 2003)**. The parental involvement directly or indirectly affected student's performance, parents' aspiration for education is associated with performance **(Anderson & Keith, 1997; Cherian, 1992; Finlayson, 1997; Reynolds & Walberg, 1992; Shumow, Vandell & Kang, 1996).**

Parental education also influences the academic performance of the students. Those parents who are educated helps in their child's learning. Parent's education is the most prominent and directly affect their child's academic performance **(Crowny & Bradley, 2002; Hoff, Laursen & Taediff, 2002; Pamela & Kean, 2005).**

Personal Factors

The personal factors of academic performance obtained at present are description of individual variables i.e., interest, intelligence, attitude, aspiration level, study habit, aptitude, motivation, self- concept and mental health of students.

Interest is the most important factor of success, it is also associated with academic performance and it is related to learning activity **(Schiefele & Csikszentmihalyi, 1995). Winteler (1992)** suggested that interest is correlated with performance in achievement tests. **Renninger, Hidi, Krapp and Renninger (1992)** reported the significant correlation between comprehensions and academic performance. Literature also sugested that schooling predicted self efficacy **(Adeyemo, 2005)**; there was a significant relationship between intrest and academic performance **(Olatoye, 2004; Olatoye & Ogunkola, 2008).**

The factor creativity is the most reliable factor to predict academic performance. The study of **Abar, Carter and Winsler, (2008); Curcio, Ferrara and De Gennaro (2006); Johnson (2008); Johnson, McGue, and Iacono (2006); Layne, Jules, Kutnick, and Layne (2008); Liew,**

McTigue, Barrois, and Hughes (2008); Mizuno et al. (2008); Moller, Stearns, Blau, and Land (2006); Parker et al., (2004); Schlee, Mullis and Shriner (2008); Thompson and Zamboanga (2004); Zhang (2004) suggested that creativity is the appropriate factor to link with academic performance. **Alam (2009)** suggested that creativity showed the positive relationship with academic performance and socio-economic status of students.

Level of aspiration is a factor which affects academic performance, everybody has a goal and they aspire to achieve their goal. Level of aspiration should be high enough to be challenging, how enough to be achievable. Scholastic achievement affects their level of aspiration **(Pal, Jain & Tiwari, 1985); Abu-Hilal (2000)** reported that level of aspiration had direct effect on performance, level of aspiration was found to have a significant effect on performance and students with higher level of aspiration had better performed. **Khan (2000)** reported that unrealistic level of aspiration adversely affected scholastic achievement and it was important factor of academic performance at any level of students. Student's aspiration levels were significantly related to educational attainment and academic performance **(Astone & McLanahan, 1991; Hanson, 1994; Horn & Carroll, 1997).**

The students attitude and study habit has been described as a belief about the subject and implicit evaluating responses, one important component of learning activities is study skills. Study skills also positively related to academic performance **(Al-Hilawani & Sartawi, 1997; Jones & Slate, 1992) and (Jones, Slate and Marini & Perez (1993)** also reported that the factor study skills describe 15 percent variance of academic grades of undergraduate students'. Several aspect of study skill demonstrates the significant relationship with academic performance in college students **(Ayodele & Adebiyi, 2013; Fazal, Hussain, Majaka & Massood, 2012; Nandita &Tanima, 2004; Novhi, 2008).**

Anxiety is also related to academic performance of students **(Seipp, 1991; Williams, 1993).** It is a general problem of daily life and plays a very critical role in human being. **Birenbaum and Nasser (1994)** reported that anxiety is negatively associated with academic performance and also similar findings of **Hancock (2001)** suggested negative effects of test anxiety on performance. Test anxious students show lower academic performance then less anxious students of similar ability **(King, Ollendick & Gullone,**

1992). The test anxiety decreases the span of attention, concentration, and memory and are responsible for low academic performance **(Devis, 2004). Rohen and Meetei (2012)** reported that the academic anxiety or state anxiety is harmful for the academic environment and performance. The test anxiety and irrelevant thought decreased the concentration and attention of students which leads to academic difficulties **(Eysenck, 2001).** Students who have high test anxiety perform poorly in academy **(Masson, et al., 2004).**

Intelligence is the most contributing factor affecting academic performance of students. Numerous studies found a relationship between intelligence and academic performance **(Devi, 1990; Kaur, 1992; Panda & Nath, 1992). Brody (1997)** reported that intelligence is positively related to academic performance. In the other study, **Chung, Dnney, Hustace and Rapport (2001)** reported that the individual differences in intelligence associated with the variation on academic performance. Intelligence is the most probable factor to predict the academic performance **(Furnham, 1995). Petrill and Wilkerson (2000)** found positive correlation between intelligence and academic performance.

Motivation is also a personal factor that is able to describe the academic performance **(Castejon & Vera-Munoz, 1996)**. Motivation directly affects the academic performance of the students **(Tucker et al., 2002)**. Students' motivation level play a significant role with academic performance **(Epstein & Sheldon, 2002; Hamilton, Hinton & Qian, 2008).**

The mental health of student's is a significant indicator of academic performance Bostani, **(Abbasabadi, 1998; Asgari, 2008; Chauhanss, 1991; Madadi, 2002; Muijs, 1997).** Nadri and Nasab (2013) found that the students who have a higher level of mental health perform better. **Barmola (2013)** findings suggested a significant positive relationship between academic performance and mental health.

The study habits of students are the most contributing factor to affect academic performance. Some studies have evidence for this factor **(Mishra, 1992; Verma & Kumar, 1999; Taplin & Jegede, 2001; Yadav & Mayuri, 2001).** Poor study habits are a cause of low academic performance **(Badhri, 1991). Alija and Blanch (2004); Cervantes, Matt, and Pechersky (1991); Watkins (1994)** found that the study habits are associated with academic performance mostly in the case of scholastic aptitudes.

The self-concept of students influences the academic performance **(Dubey & Mishra, 1997; Ford & Grantham, 2003)**. Self-concept can be considered as essentially independent. Most of the studies supported the contention that positive self-concepts correlated with academic performance **(Bruns, 1992; Cherian & Moeketsi, 1998; Diaz, 1998; Ford, 1996; Geetha, 2000; Kumar, 1999; Schunk, 1998; Srivastava, 1992; Supplee, 1990; Van Boxtel & Monks, 1992)**. Self-concept found a significant association with high and low achievers. **(Tiwari & Bansal, 1994; Pujar, Caonkar & Sharma, 1997)**. Several researches show that the higher levels of self-concept is correlated with educational outcomes of students **(Marsh, 1990; Marsh & Craven, 1997; Marsh & Hau, 2003).**

Personality and its Relation to Academic Performance

Personality is a diverse and complex behavioural reaction pattern and represents the individual's whole concept. It is the most important and noticeable part of an individual's psychological life. "Personality is dynamic and organized set of characteristics possessed by a person that uniquely influences his or her cognitions, emotions, interpersonal orientations motivations, and behaviours in various situations. Its define that how persons unique and different form each other's." According to **Allport (1948)** "personality is a dynamic organization within the individual of those psychophysical systems that determine his unique adjustment to his environment" **(Mangal, 2010 p. 393)**. "Personality is the organized developing system within the individual that represents the collective action of that individual's major psychological subsystems" **(Mayer, 2007, p.14)**.

The personality of an individual depends on their characteristics, intelligence, aptitude, interest, attitude, ideas, expectation, thought and behaviour and it's determined by the biological and environmental factors also. In the area of educational psychology, the student personality and their performance is the most important issue. Nowadays students face many psychosocial problems in everyday life i.e., anxiety to give best in institutions, fear for examinations, frustration, peer pressure, and parental expectation, etc. They try to resolve their problems in various situations. When they are not overcome with their problems they feel frustration or depression and it affects their personality, therefore, influence their academic performance. In the present circumstance many countries provide the knowledge of personality development to students for their success of life. **Kuppuswamy (2000)** suggested that a healthy personality development in students is the fundamental goal of education because the students' academic performance also affect their personality. The different type of personality present at birth and education cannot change but the personality influence human performance in every phase of life; good personality affects the mental and physical health of students' and ar responsible for better educational outcomes. Personality is the most significant predictor of academic performance of the students **(AlQaisy & Khaffash, 2012; Basher & Malik, 2012; Busato et al., 1999; Nehara, 2014; Polleys, 2001; Rindermann & Neubauer, 2001; Varghese, 2005).**

In a recent personality research, the basic five factors of personality widely used are neuroticism, extraversion, openness to experience, agreeableness and conscientiousness **(Costa & McCrae, 1992).** The five factors of personality are a strong representation for normal personality **(Tokar, Fischer, & Subich, 1998).**

In psychological research, the five factors of personality were capable to describe human personality pattern and lot of psychologists accepted that the five factors are the main structure of personality. These five personality factors influences the academic performance **(Safara, 2006; Salehi, Khak & Alam, 2013)**. The five factors of personality traits has a strong relation with academic performance **(Poropat, 2009)**. Several studies reported the association of five personality factors and student's academic success **(Allik, 2007; DeYoung, 2010; Komarraju, Karau, & Schmeck, 2009; Kumari, 2014; Melissa, O'Connor & Sampo, 2007; O'Connor & Paunonen, 2008; Peteska, 2006; Rogers, 2005; Rosander, 2013; Rothstein Paunonen, Rush & King, 1994; Veroude et al., 2013;).** The academic performance of the students is influenced by the five factor model of personality **(Nguyen, Fraccastora 2006; Shokri, Daneshvarpour & Askari, 2008). Pornsakulvanich et al. (2012)** studied the effect of five personality traits and cognitive affective academic performance and the findings indicated that conscientiousness, openness and agreeableness predict cognitive performance and extraversion openness, agreeableness and conscientiousness predict the affective academic performance. The whole personality traits found the better predictor of academic performance.

Mustaffa et al. (2012) reported that the openness, agreeableness and conscientiousness differ significantly on the basis of gender upon academic success in medical students. **Chamorro-Premuzic and Furnham (2003); Laidra, Pullmamm and Allik (2006); Troncone, Drammis and Labella (2014); Petska, Bruning and Scheel (2006)** contribution suggested that the big five personality traits are a significant predictor of academic success.

The five factor personalities i.e., Neuroticism, Extraversion, Openness, Agreeableness and Conscientiousness influence the academic performance **(Koning et al., 2012). Diseth (2003)** reported that the factors neuroticism, openness negatively correlated with academic performance and agreeableness positively associated with academic performance. Neuroticism correlated with academic achievement, particularly for the factor of impulsivity and anxiety **(Kuncel et al., 2005).** Neuroticism correlated with study attitudes in school children and university students also **(Busato, Prins, Elshout, & Hamaker, 2000; Crede & Kuncel, 2008; Heaven, Mak, Barry & Ciarrochi, 2002). O'Conner and Paunonen (2007) and Trapmann Hell, Hirn and Schuler (2007)** reported the negative correlation between extraversion and academic success. **Furnham and Chamorro-Premuzic (2004)** found that the adolescents and adults subjects with highly extrovert show low academic performance than introvert. Some studies show that the extrovert performed better **(Chamorro-Premuzic & Furnham, 2003; Chowdhury, 2006; Furnham & Medhurst, 1995; Robinson, Gabriel, & Katchan, 1993) Hakimi et al., (2011)** reported that the extraversion and neuroticism are significantly negative predictors of academic performance of university students. **Wright (2008)** indicated that openness, agreeableness, conscientiousness, and emotional stability are positively related to academic performance. **Furnham et al. (2009)** reported that the agreeableness, conscientiousness and extraversion show the significant relation with academic performance.

Openness is the most important personality factor that predicts academic performance **(Komarraju, Karau, & Schmeck, 2009; Laidra, et. al. 2007).** It is related to better scores in vocabulary and general knowledge **(Ackerman & Heggestad, 1997; Ashton, Lee, Vernon, & Jang, 2000)** and also positively related to academic performance **(Geisler-Brenstein & Schmeck, 1996; Komarraju, Karau & Schmeck, 2009). Rothstein Paunonen, Rush and King (1994)** found a significant relation between the trait agreeableness and academic performance. Agreeableness show significant positive relation with academic performance. **(Farsides & Woodfield, 2003; Gray & Watson, 2002). Komarraju, Karau, Schmeck and Avdic (2011)** reported that the big five factor i.e. agreeableness and conscientiousness positively related to learning style and its influence on academic performance.

Komarraju and Karau (2005) indicated that openness and conscientiousness is a significant predictor of academic performance. **Busato, Prins, Elshout and Hamaker (1999); Chamorro-Premuzic and Furnham, (2003); Chowdhury (2006); Laidra, Pullman and Allik (2006); O'Connor and Paunonen (2007); Rindermann and Neubauer (2001)** suggested the GPA has positive relation with Conscientiousness trait of personality. **Duff et al., (2004)** research show that the factor conscientiousness is a significant predictor of academic performance in university students. Conscientiousness trait of big five is more effective in time management practices, which is a responsible factor for academic success **(McKenzie & Gow, 2004). Waterman and Funder (2007)** found that the factor conscientiousness is a predictor of college performance. **Lievens, Cortsier, Defruyt and DeMaessneer (2002)** found that conscientiousness and extraversion was a successful predictor of school performance, but the agreeableness factor shows no significant relation. **Ferguson, Sanders, O Hehir and James (2000)** found that the personality trait conscientiousness had a significant variance upon academic performance.

Morningness-Eveningness Preference and its Relation to Academic Performance

Human beings prefer their alertness early or delayed. This characteristic is called chronotype. The continuum is often referred to as "Morningness-Eveningness" preference. The people who wake up early and are more active in the first part of the day are called morning type 'larks' and those people who are more active in late evening and also prefer to go to bed late are called evening types 'owls' **(Voinescu, Bogdan Ioan, 2010)**. Morningness-eveningness preference (circadian typology) is capable of explaining the variation in the expression of behavioural and biological patterns of human being as 'morning type', 'evening type' and 'intermediate type' as a stable characteristic **(Adan et al., 2008, 2010).** These characteristics in human nature have been most widely investigated by **(Achari and Pati (2010);**

Giannotti, Cortesi and Sepastiani (2002); Harad, Morisone and Takeuchi (2002); Harington (1994); Lima, Medeiros and Araujo (2002); Pati, Chandrawanshi and Reinberg (2001).

Circadian rhythms influence the physiological and psychological functions of individual's and various factors of their life i.e., study, eating, exercise, work capacity and behaviour. It's only affected by the daily cycles (24 hours) approach **(Cavallera & Giudici, 2008). Horne and Ostberg (1976)** reported that the people who have morning types show higher temperature with earlier peak time as compared to evening types and they went to sleep and awoke earlier. The individual's characteristic shows some biological correlates and that appears to correlates highly with the performance in morningness-eveningness preference.

Humans are generally active in the first part of the day i.e., morning time as compared to evening and afternoon time. In the Indian context, lifestyle of many cultures and families awake in early morning and the tendency or thinking of the one and all, the morning time is the best period for learning and those people who studied in the morning time perform better, and most of the students prefer to go to bed earlier and awoke early in the morning for the studies but in the present circumstances the students tendency is different in this way of learning preference. The morningness-eveningness preference of students affects their academic performance **(Goldstein, Hahn, Hasher, Wiprzycka & Zelazo, 2006; Hines, 2004; Ishihara et al, 1990)**.

Most of the studies suggested that the school day starts too early for adolescent students. The findings of **Hasher, Goldstein and May (2005); Itons-Peterson, Rocchi, West, McLellan and Hackney (1998); May (1999); Randal and Frech, (2009)** suggested that the adult student show better performance in the morning than later in the day and evening time show bad performance than the morning and afternoon time. Morning type students performed better than evening type students **(Besoluk, 2010 & Besoluk, Onder & Deveci 2011)**. Eveningness was negatively associated with academic performance and positively associated with the individual's cognitive ability. Morningness shows a positive relation to academic indicators and negative association to cognitive ability **(Preckel, Lipnevich, Schneider & Roberts, 2011)**. Franzisp, Anastasiya, Sandra and Richard (2011) found that eveningness was negatively related to academic performance and morningness show positive relation with academic performance **(Roberts, Roberts, & Duong, 2009).**

Gender and its relation to Academic Performance

Gender is a biogenic factor giving scope for identifiable appropriate differences to the anatomy and physiology of male and female, gender is the typical combination of characteristics that generally differentiate male from female. Due to their inner differences, the pattern of socialization has also been found different for the male and female person in Indian and other cultural set up. Gender difference plays a vital role in all the affairs of human behaviour and so does in respect of their academic performance. Several studies indicated the gender gap in academic performance **(Ferguson & Harwood, 1997; Hillman, 2003; Praat, 1999; Weaver-Hightower, 2003).** Educational researches indicated that the females perform better than males **(Alton Lee & Praat; Amitava, Maojit, Saawata and Braja, 2010; Escribano, Iaz-Morales, Delgdo & Collado, 2011; Linn, 2006; Mirza & Malik, 2000; Mullis et al., 2003; Rana, 2000; Spelk, 2005).**

Several studies provided the evidence that boys perform better in cognitive affective and psychomotor skills and academic performance than females **(Aguele & Uhumniah, 2008; Amitava, Manojit, Saswata & Braja, 2010; Billings, 2000; Croxford, 2002; Hyde & McKinley, 1997; Kolawole, 2007).**

On the contrary, studies show that the academic performance of the students do not get influenced by the gender **(Arigbabu & Mji, 2004; Bilesanmi-Awoderu, 2006; Din, Ming & Esther, 2004; Freedman, 2002; Gupta, Sharma and Gupta, 2012; Oludipe, 2012 & Sungur &Tekkaya, 2003).**

Academic Performance in Engineering Students

Academic performance is the most important aspect of education. It is the key to judging the individual's potentiality and ability. Academic performance has a vital place in education in the students learning process. In the field of engineering, academic performance is the most important aspect of their education and also their career pathway. The engineering student's profile of study is different from those student's who are in other disciplines. Engineering students must be capable and have relevant knowledge of physics, mathematics, and life science in order to understand formulates and solve engineering problems. Most of the studies suggested a strong relation between engineering course, ability and academic success **(Astin & Astin, 1992; Halper, 2000; Lubinski, 2010; Zhang, Anderson, Ohland, Corter & Thorndyke, 2004)**. Engineering is the most challenging undergraduate course; a lot of students perform badly and fail because the course requires solid mathematical skills and better understanding of elementary concepts and principles in the field **(Self, Wood, & Hansen, 2004)**. The predicting academic performance in engineering students is helpful to designing and implementing academic interventions to increase learning in this crucial course. Many factors influence both male and female student's performance. **(Miika, Kirsi & Seppo, 2008)** studied that the insufficient skills in basic mathematics problems for students majoring in engineering affected their academic performance. In a engineering course, the high self-efficacy show low anxiety and better working style and focus and its influence on the academic performance of the students. An engineering institute demands more adjustment by the students, most of the difficulties and critical situations the students faced in their institution and these types of factors affected student's adjustment and personality which consequently influence the academic performance.

In the present circumstances, engineering students performance is the most significant concept for study in the education and personality psychology and the factor circadian rhythm and personality is the most contributing factor for their academic performance. Gender difference is also associated with the engineering students' personality and its relation with academic performance.

Education qualities play a significant role in the development of any nation. It is an unique investment and academic performance is an essential part of it. Our society is changing everyday and also demands high achievers. Success is considered as the highest expectation to provide challenges and encouragement essential to push the student for highest performance and everyone is encouraged to succeed and is considered an essential member of society.

In this competitive world academic success is the key to students' success in future. It has been an important goal of the educational process in which every person is expected to perform better in all cultures. A careful observation of the existing literature on academic performance revealed that academic performance largely depends on parenting practices, intelligence, study habits, motivation, level of aspiration, self regulation learning, etc. In this connection it was thought appropriate that some personality factors, morningness-eveningnesss preference affect the academic performance of the technical students. This important aspect has not been given due attention by the researchers, especially in Chhattisgarh state it has been almost neglected. Therefore, the present study is undertaken with a view to examine the role of different personality factors namely, neuroticism, extraversion, openness, agreeableness and conscientiousness, morningness-eveningness preference and gender on academic performance of the engineering students.

Chapter Two

A COMPREHENSIVE REVIEW OF LITERATURE

Literature review is the most significant part of any scientific research. It provides the researchers an insight into the problem and also helps to investigate for the formulation of hypothesis. Hence, the main purpose of the review related literature is to have an understanding of the trend of research in the field and regarding any space in research. In this section, the researcher has attempted to include the earlier concluded investigations within India and other countries. These studies will help the researcher to provide knowledge about those factors which affect the academic performance of the students. To understand the factors that influence the academic performance it can be categorized into three main groups, i.e., Biological Factors, Psychological Factors and Social-Demographic Factors.

Biological Factors: Biological factors include the birth order, cognitive ability, sleep pattern, etc.

Psychological Factors: Psychological factors include intelligence, motivation, study habits, anxiety, self-concept, interest, level of aspiration, cognitive ability, personality, emotional intelligence, etc.

Socio-Demographic Factors: Socio-Demographic factors include parental education, peer group, family environment, parental involvement, socio-economic status, gender, locale school environment, etc.

Biological Factors – Biological factors of any individual affect their academic performance such as birth order, cognitive ability and sleep pattern. These factors affect the mental functioning and cognitive development of individuals and also significantly influence the academic performance of the students. These variables along with some other variables are discussed below

Birth Order

Birth Order of the child has a significant association to their academic performance. **Cherian (1990)** studied the relationship between birth order and academic achievement of pupils in Transkei, South Africa. Results indicated a significant negative association with academic performance students and their academic success. **Paulhus Trapnell and Chen (1999)** findings suggested that the first born child shows more academic achievement as compared to younger siblings.

Kumar (2011) examined the relationship between birth order and academic performance of management students. A significant relation was found between academic performance and birth order and the result indicated that the second born child performed better than the other birth order.

Tshui and Caiilan (2011)) investigated the birth order effect on personality and academic performance. Samples of 30 first born, 30 middle born, 30 last born and 30 only children who shared the mean age of 20 years were recruited into the study. The results indicated that participants of different birth position did not differ significantly in terms of personality and academic achievement and Pearson's Correlation showed that extraversion correlated positively with academic performance.

Chronotype

Chronotype is an individual difference characteristic reflecting the time of day at which individuals are "at their best" **(Guthrie, 1995)**. Though some people prefer to wake up early in the morning and are most alert in the first part of the day, others prefer to wake up later, as their peak time of the day is in the evening, and they prefer to go to bed late at night **(Cofer et al., 1999; Tankova. Adan, Buela-Casal, 1994).**

BaHammam, Al-Faris, Shaikh and Saeed (2006) studied the association of sleep problems and sleep habits with performance. Result indicated that the students who have sleep problems and poor sleep habits negatively influence the academic performance.

Daniel, Kendra, Adam, Kevin and Brandy (2006) investigated that comprehensive assessment of psycho-social functioning and academic performance in relation to Circadian phase preference in a US sample of undergraduate college students. Findings suggested that the female show greater morning preference than men, and senior students show greater morning preference than freshmen. Circadian phase preference, fatigue, perceived stress, depression, anxiety, and substance use were assessed cross-sectional and grade point average was assessed. Evening phase preference was related to higher levels of fatigue, alcohol and caffeine use, and worse academic performance than morning or intermediate phase preference.

David, Constanze, Lynn, Wiprzycka, and Philip (2006) studied the influence of fluid and crystallized intelligence to Morning and Evening-type adolescents' performance. Result indicated that the evening type have more maladaptive behaviour and also show the risk for poor academic performance.

Randal and Frech (2009) investigated that the young people who shift their time-of-day preferences affect the performances. Result indicated that the people with morning preferences performed better in academic performance.

Parker (2009) studied the consequences of the adolescent's Circadian shift and its relation to learning. The research reported differences between morning and afternoon classes apart from gender that showed the significant difference. Findings suggested that the four group's i.e., morning learners in morning classes, morning learners in afternoon classes, afternoon learners in morning classes, and afternoon learners in afternoon classes noted that the three groups with an afternoon component in their learning outscored the one group with no afternoon influence in their learning.

Besoluk (2010) investigated that the influence of morningness–eveningness preference on academic performance in a standardised university entrance examination. Results indicated a significant association of morningness-eveningness preference and university entrance examination scores. In addition "morning" type students performed better as compared to "intermediate" type and "evening" type students.

Besoluk, Onder and Deveci (2011) investigated the influence of Circadian preferences of students to their academic performance. Findings suggested that the different class times affected a student's achievement and examined the performance of students, thus the students who have morning preference achieved higher scores than either those with evening or intermediate preference.

Escribano, Diaz-Morales, Delgdo and Collado (2011) studied the influence of chronotype, and optimal sleep duration on academic performance. Results indicated that the chronotype, and optimal sleep duration positively associated with academic performance, evening-types perform worse in school.

Franzis, Anastasiya, Sandra and Richard (2011) examined the relationships between morningness and cognitive ability and academic achievement. Findings suggested that the eveningness was found to be positively related to individual's cognitive ability, yet negatively related to indicators of academic achievement and morningness showed the negative relationship with cognitive ability and a positive association with academic performance.

Cognitive Ability

Cognitive ability is the most powerful predictor of academic performance. **Little, Das (1993)** studied the relationship between performance and cognitive ability test and the findings revealed that the higher order ability predicts the academic performance.

Hatlie (1996); Masten and Coatsworth (1998); Wang et al. (1994) found that the three clusters of individual skills, i.e., cognitive and meta cognitive skills, social skills and self-management skills were responsible for a student's school success. The cognitive and meta cognition skills include skills like goal setting progress monitoring and memory skills, social skills include interpersonal skills, social problem solving and teamwork skills and the self-management skills like managing attention, motivation and anger influence the student's success. These skills were the most powerful predictor of longer school success.

Hunt (1995) studied the predicting effects of mental ability on academic performance. Findings revealed a strong correlation between academic performance and mental ability.

Wadsworth, Defries, Fulker and Plomin (1995) examined the influence of academic performance and cognitive ability, the findings revealed that mathematics achievement 54% correlated with cognitive ability, verbal comprehension 60% correlated with academic performance, 64% correlation between perceptual organization and academic performance, and reading recognition 63% correlated with mathematics performance. The findings also suggested that covariance among reading and mathematics performance was independent of cognitive ability.

Kush (1996) investigated the relationship of field dependence to task of cognitive ability and academic performance and the findings suggested that reasoning ability of the students is the best predictor of academic performance.

Richard (1997) studied the relationship between cognitive ability learning related behaviour, achievement, responsibility and academic performance. Results found that the learning is related to behaviours and their interaction with cognitive ability predicted the academic performance.

King (2000); Furnham, Chomorro-Premuzic and McDougall (2003) investigated the relation between mental ability and high school result, findings suggested a significant correlation with performance.

Yen, Konold and McDermott (2004) found a meaningful variance upon academic performance and non-intellectual factors. Non-intellectual factors are a significant predictor of academic performance. **James (2004)** examined the academic performance of students predicted by the cognitive ability and multiple regression results revealed that the cognitive ability of adolescents accounted for 28% variance upon academic performance and findings also suggested that cognitive ability, aggression and work drive were a good predictor of academic performance.

Whereas some studies shows Deangelis (2003); Grigorenko and Sternberg (2001); Mattern and Show (2010); Sanford (2009) found that the cognitive ability cannot be a suitable factor to understanding student performance.

Rohde, Eileen, Thompson and Anne (2007) examined the relationship between academic performance and specific and general cognitive ability. Specific cognitive ability such as working memory, spatial ability, and processing speed predicted the academic performance and the general cognitive ability also predict academic performance after conditioning the specific cognitive ability.

Crede and Kuncel (2008) revealed that the factor of cognitive ability shows the strong relation with academic performance. Cognitive ability and positive thinking variables (hope, self-esteem, and attribution style) predict the highest degree of academic performance. The results also reveal that the intelligence and positive thinking play an important role in predicting the academic performance.

Alloway, Elliott and Place (2010) concluded that the students who have poor working memory perform poorly in their learning outcomes and especially poor in reading and mathematics performance. **Polderman, Boomsma, Bartels, Verhulst and Huizink (2010)** found that working memory and attention deficits was associated with poor arithmetic and reading performance.

Phillipson and Sivanes (2010) studied the cognitive ability and parental involvement and expectation predicts the academic performance. The findings indicated that the parental, home and school involvement and parental beliefs about their child's ability was responsible for academic score and IQ score is the valuable predictor of academic performance in English and Mathematics.

Bangirana et al. (2011) examined the effects of cognitive ability and academic performance result revealed that attention has shown a borderline significant effect on academic performance and no significant difference between cognitive ability and academic performance. Diniz, **Dias and Silva (2011)** studied the effect of socio-culture background and cognitive ability on academic performance. Findings suggested that socio-cultural background influence the cognitive ability and it affects the academic performance of students and results also found that the cognitive ability show mediation effect of socio-cultural background and academic performance in the higher secondary school students.

Chen, Hwang, Yeh and (2012) studied the effect of specific area of cognitive ability and grades in a different field of self-concept and findings suggested a significant positive path correlation between cognitive ability and self-concept in the same area and between these two constructs of grades indirect effect and cross area effects of ability or grades on academic self-concept were negatively related.

Robertson and Maree (2012) investigated the mediating effect of learning style and strategies on the relation among cognitive ability and academic performance. Results revealed that the higher cognitive ability and learning strategies play an important role to predict the academic performance. Learning strategies were found, there was no significant relation with academic performance and they also found that rehearsal as a mediator in the association between cognitive ability and cognitive ability indirectly affects the academic performance.

Thayer, Kido (2012) studied the relationship of cognitive genesis ability and performance and result revealed that ability predicts the highest academic performance. **Dzulkifi (2012)** studied the effect of personality and mental ability on academic performance and results indicated a significant association between personality and cognitive ability on low achievers.

Fin, et al. (2014) examined that the cognitive skills predict the academic performance and the result also revealed positive effect of school attendance, achievement and cognitive skill had showed no significant effect on academic performance.

Nutrition level

Nutrition level of students directly or indirectly affects their academic performance **(Brown, Beardslee and Prothrow-Sith (2008)** pointed out that the poor nutrition level was responsible for illness like headaches, week eyesight and stomach-aches and it results in absenteeism and influence the academic performance.

Fioorence, Asbridge and Veuqelers (2008) examined the effect of diet quality on academic performance of United States students. Result indicated that the students who have poor diet quality perform poorly on academic performance. Chinyoka (2014) studied the effect of nutrition on academic performance of students. Result suggested that poor nutrition affects the academic performance.

Sleep Pattern

The most reliable findings suggested that less sleep duration is positively associated with lower level of academic performance **(Medeiros et al., 2001; Trockel et al., 2000).**

AnaLigia et al. (2001) studied the relationship between sleep walk cycle and academic performance in medical students. Results indicated that the students who have evening type or moderate evening type show more sleep disturbance and result also suggested that the irregular sleep and chronotype influence the quality of the sleep walk cycle and influences the learning performance of college students.

Walter,Franklin and Barlow (2001) studied the sleep habits and pattern of college student's performance. Result indicated that the sleep disturbance was more in female and the harmful effect of sleep problem influenced the academic performance.

Bruni, et. al. (2006) examined the relationship between academic performance and sleep temperament in school students. Result indicated that the sleep pattern and temperament are a most significant factor for academic performance.

Blunden and Chervin (2007) studied the association of the student's sleep problems and academic outcomes. Result suggested that the sleep problems are responsible for problematic behaviour and poor academic performance also.

El-Sheikh, Buckhalt, Keller, Cummings and Acebo, (2007) examined the relationship of sleep disruptions, emotional insecurity in family and academic performance. Results indicated that the children who have emotional insecurity reported sleep disturbance and quality of sleep were intervening variables in the relations between insecurity and academic performance. The effect of disrupted sleep is responsible for poor academic output. Result suggested that the family and sleep functioning is the predictor of student's outcomes.

Pagel, Forister and Kwiatkowki (2007) investigated the effect of socio-economic variables on academic performance and examined the relationship between sleep disturbance and academic performance of adolescents. Results indicated that the lower level of family income reported poor academic performance and also sleep disturbance significantly affects the academic performance.

Schmidt, Collette, Cajochen and Peigneux (2007) studied the relationship between the sleep–wake cycle and cognitive performance. Results suggested that the duration of sleep, difficulty, and cognitive domain of a task influence the sleep–wake cycle on cognitive performance.

Johnston, Grastudied, Dohnt, Billows and Mccapdisar (2010) found the relationship between fluid intelligence, sleep pattern and academic performance. The fluid intelligence predicts the moderate relationship between adolescent sleep and academic performance.

Lowry, Dean and Manders (2010) examined the association between sleep quantity and academic performance of college students. Results indicated a significant positive association quantity of sleep per night and GPA.

Sweileh et al. (2011) studied the effect of sleep habits and sleep problems in undergraduate college students. Results indicated that most of the students reported the parasomnia disorder and sleep quality was reported as "poor" in only 9.8% and was significantly associated with sleep latency, frequency of nocturnal awakenings, time of going to bed and nightmares, but not with academic performance. Finally, the result suggested that the sleep quality have showed no significant association with academic performance.

Psychological Factors – Psychological factors significantly influence the academic performance. The psychological state of any individual is the most important to determine how they perform better or worse in academic institutions. The psychological factors such as motivation, level of aspiration, anxiety, intelligence, study habits and personality are the most contributing psychological factors influencing academic performance. These factors along with some other factors are discussed below:

Adjustment

Chen, Rubin and Li (1997) studied the relationship between academic performance, social adjustment in Chinese students, and result indicated that social adjustment is a significant predictor of academic performance. Social competence and peer acceptance affect the student's social adjustment and it affects the student's academic performance.

Adjustment is critical for academic success. Poor college adjustment correlates with poor academic performance, and poor success in future life. **Adler, Raju, Beveridge, Wang, Zhu and Zimmermann (2008)** examined the effect of college adjustment and quality of life on academic performance. Results revealed that the physical and emotional factors affect the adjustment of college students and their higher graduation academic performance and future success.

Saikia and Samad (2013) examined the relationship between academic performance and adjustment of students. Findings indicated a negative correlation between academic performance and student's adjustment. Urban students have more adjustment problem than the rural area students and no gender difference was found significant.

Anxiety

The academic performance of the students is poorly affected by the anxiety in our society. **Eysenck (2001)** reveals that anxiety generates irrelevant thoughts and decreased attention and concentration and is responsible for academic difficulties. The effect of test anxiety and evaluation threats on student's performance and motivation at post-secondary level found significant results that the high level of anxiety was responsible for poor performance and less motivated to learning **(Hancock, 2001). Hembree (1998); Seipp (1991)** found a negative relationship between test anxiety and academic performance among college students.

Henry and Dennis (1992) studied the effect of acute test taking anxiety on academic performance of second year medical students. The result indicated a significant correlation between acute test anxiety and medical examiners performance. **Shunmuga (1995)** investigated the effect of anxiety on academic performance. Results indicated a negative correlation between anxiety and academic performance of the students. Student's who have low anxiety perform better as compared to student's who have high level of anxiety. **Lalis (1997)** studied the effect of examination anxiety on science performance of the students. Findings indicated that the examination anxiety is a harmful factor for academic performance.

Cassady and Johnson (2002) examined the relationship between cognitive test anxiety and academic performance and results found that anxiety explained a significant negative impact on academic performance. **Sud and Prabha (2003)** examined the relationship between perfectionism, test procrastination, test anxiety and academic performance in high school students. Result indicated that the academic performance negatively related to self-oriented thoroughness, test anxiety, test procrastination and emotional stability.

Davis (2004) demonstrates that higher secondary students with high test anxiety, decrease attention, memory and concentration and is responsible for low academic performance. Higher level of test anxiety in high school students had shown poor school performance **(Masson et al., 2004).**

Chepell et el. (2005) studied test anxiety and academic performance of graduate and undergraduate students and result indicated a negative association between test anxiety and academic performance.

Needham (2006) reported that anxiety disrupts memory and concentration and as a result leads to low academic performance. The effect of test anxiety on student's performance and result indicated that anxiety was related to academic performance **(Nicholson, 2009). Sud and Sujata (2006)** studied the academic performance relation with examination anxiety, self-handicapping and study habits. Result suggested that the self-handicapping and anxiety show negative influence on academic performance.

Gautam and Swati (2008) examined the relationship of academic performance of high school students with test anxiety and level of aspiration. Result indicated that the academic performance of the students negatively affects the test anxiety and level of aspiration also show negative effect on academic performance.

Oludipe (2009) investigated the influence of test anxiety on academic performance on secondary school physics, numerical students and result found that low test anxious student's performance was better than high test anxious students on both numerical and physics.

Ndirangu, et al. (2009) examined the relationship between test anxiety and academic performance in the students of Kenya. Students experience high level of anxiety before the examinations in every subject. The result indicated that the teachers do not sufficient help students to manage with test anxiety. So the relationship between test anxiety and academic performance was not found, also result revealed that the boys and girls both are equally affected by the test anxiety.

Rana and Mahmaood (2010) investigated the relationship between test anxiety and academic performance and result revealed that test anxiety is responsible for student's low performance. **Yousefi et al. (2010)** examined the relationship between test anxiety and academic achievement and result revealed a significant correlation between test anxiety and academic performance.

Putwaina, et al. (2010) studied the relationship between cognitive distortions, test anxiety and examination performance. Result indicated that the significant association between the components of test anxiety worry, bodily system and academic performance.

Nadeen, Ali, Maqbool and Zaidi (2012) investigated the impact of anxiety on the academic performance of students having some mental difficulties at university level. The result indicated that the increased anxiety level explains the decrease in academic performance of students.

Al-Qaisy (2011) examined the relationship between depression, anxiety and academic performance among university students. The result indicated a positive association between academic performance and anxiety and negative association with depression.

Creativity

Creativity is a relevant factor to predict students' academic performance. The study of **Abar, Carter and Winsler, (2008); Curcio, Ferrara and De Gennaro (2006); Johnson (2008); Johnson, McGue, and Iacono (2006); Layne, Jules, Kutnick, and Layne (2008); Liew, McTigue, Barrois, and Hughes (2008); Mizuno et al. (2008); Moller, Stearns, Blau, and Land (2006); Schlee, Mullis and Shriner (2008); Thompson and Zamboanga (2004); Zhang (2004)** suggested that creativity is a appropriate factor to link with academic performance.

V De Fruyt and Mervielde (1996) indicated that the cre¬ative and imaginative nature is a drawback for academic success of any individual. **Komarraju, Karau, & Schmeck (2008)** reported that creativity is not a reliable factor to predict academic performance. **Naderi, Abdullah, Aizan, Sharir, Kumar (2009)** studied the relationship of creativity with academic performance. The result indicated no significant prediction of students academic success.

Alam (2009) examined the effect of creativity and socio-economic status of students' academic performance. Findings suggested that creativity show a positive relationship with academic performance and socio-economic status of students.

Emotional Intelligence

Academic success depends on the intelligence and also it is affected by the emotional intelligence of the students **(Golman, 1995)**. **Abisamra (2000)** found that the emotional intelligent significantly correlated with group performance and academic performance. The findings of **Schuttle et al. (1998) and Tapia (1998)** revealed a significant association between emotional intelligence and scholastic aptitude test.

Parker, Summerfeldt, Hogan and Majeski (2004) investigated the relationship of emotional intelligence with academic success. Result found that the different dimensions of emotional intelligence strongly related to academic success.

Petridesa, Fredericksonb and Furnhamb (2004) examined the role of trait emotional intelligence in academic performance. Result showed that trait emotional intelligence as being a moderator of cognitive ability and academic performance.

Parker, Duffy, Wood, Bond and Hogan (2009) studied the effect of emotional intelligence on the successful change from high school to university. Results revealed that the students who have greater emotional and social competencies show significantly higher levels of academic success. These findings suggested that the role of emotional intelligence is very important for successful transition from high school to university.

Ogundokun and Ibadan (2010) investigated the moderating effect of emotional intelligence, age and academic motivation on academic performance. Result indicated emotional intelligence, age and academic motivation as a powerful predictor of academic performance.

Shabana and Rani (2013) studied the effect of emotional intelligence of higher secondary students on academic performance. Result indicated that emotional intelligence show significant difference in higher secondary students academic success.

Intelligence

Intelligence is the most significant factor affecting a student's performance. Several researches investigated the association between intelligence and academic performance **(Allik & Realo, 1997; Gagne& St Pere, 2002; Kobal & Musek, 2001; Koke & Vernon, 2003; Kossowska, 1999; Smith, Smith & Doobbs, 1991; Saleh, I. at el., 2001). Rapport, Denney and Hustace (2001)** found individual difference in intelligence was related to academic performance.

Stipek and Gralinkis (1996) studied the relationship among students belief about intelligence and effort goal orientation, self-report learning strategies and academic performance. Result indicated that the belief on intelligence had a global effect on academic performance. Student's belief to intelligence is fixed and affection performance is negatively associated with academic performance.

Begum and Phukan (2001) investigated the association between academic performance and intelligence in boys and girls. Result indicated that the intelligence of the students was positively associated with academic performance. The result also suggested the girls correlation with intelligence and academic performance was greater than the boys.

Chomorro-Premuzic, Furnham and McDougall (2003) studied the relationship between five factors of personality, cognitive abilities and intelligence. The result indicated that the university students who are conscientiousness were more likely to think about intelligence and students who are low conscientiousness are more likely to believe that intelligence is stable. Conscientiousness was positively related to academic performance.

Harris (2004) examined the relation between intelligence, creativity; achievement and openness to experience and result found that intelligence have shown a moderate positive correlation with academic performance. **Begum and Phukan (2005)** examined the association of academic performance with intelligence and result indicated that the intelligence of the students positively correlated with academic performance.

Laidra, Pullman and Allik (2006) studied the predicting effect of intelligence and personality on academic success in the sample of 3618 college students. Result found that intelligence is the strongest predictor of student's performance. **Colom and Mendoza (2006)** examined that intelligence predicts scholastic performance by socio-economic status and result revealed that intelligence predicts the children's scholastic performance.

Deary, Strand, Smith and Fernandes (2007) investigated the relationship of intelligence with academic success and result revealed that intelligence shows strong correlation with academic performance. **Road and Thompson (2007)** examined the predicting effects on academic performance with cognitive ability and result found that the general cognitive ability predicts the academic performance.

Massey and Ehrmann (2008) found that highly intelligent students show higher academic performance than student's with low level of intelligence. **Gurrrubasappa (2009)** studied intelligence and self-concept as a correlate of academic performance and result showed that intelligence and self-concept highly correlated with academic performance.

Habibollah et al. (2009) studied the gender difference in creative perception of undergraduate students and result reveals no significant correlation between intelligence and academic performance.

Naderi (2010) examined the relation between academic performance and intelligence and result found that the correlation between intelligence and performance is difficult. A comparative study of intelligence and academic performance of Tibetan and Kashmiri students was done and result found a significant difference between intelligence and performance among these groups **(Mudasir & Yatu, 2012).**

Level of Aspiration

Abu Hilal (2000) studied the structural model of attitude towards school subjects, academic performance and result revealed that attitude toward school influences performance. Level of aspiration had shown a significant effect on achievement and mediated between attitudes and performance.

Vaidya (2006) examined the comparison between academic performance aspirations of higher secondary student's of formal and non-formal education. Result revealed significant differences in academic performance between the student's studying during formal and non-formal education in the area of reading comprehension, writing and grammar and vocabulary.

Motivation

Motivation is the key to effective learning and good discipline. Many studies found no significant association between academic motivation and performance **(Katyal & Bindra, 1995; Ray, Lipika, Bibi & Manjula, 1994). Pretorius (1998)** found that the lake of motivation is responsible for school fatigue, leaving school, bunking, underachievement and problematic behaviour.

Tella (2007) investigated the impact of motivation and academic performance and learning outcomes and result indicated that motivation is a significant variable of interest of academic work and improved academic performance. Academic motivation is also positively related to academic performance **(Robinson, 2003; Steinmayr & Spinath, 2009).**

Nagarathanamma and Thirumala (2007) studied the relationship of mental health, achievement motivation and academic performance. Result indicated no significant relationship between academic motivation and success.

Pandey (2008) examined the relationship with academic motivation parental background and student's academic. The positive correlation found that the academic motivation, academic performance and working parents significantly influence the academic performance and motivation, on the other hand, parents qualification show no significant relation with academic performance and academic motivation.

Kusarkar, et al. (2011) studied the motivational effect on academic performance of medical university student's and results demonstrated that motivation shows the positive relation with academic performance. **Gupta**

(2014) examined the effect of self-concept, achievement motivation and socio-demographical factor on academic performance. Result revealed no significant difference between self-concept and academic success but achievement motivation was highly correlated with academic performance of the students.

Personality

Many studies in the field of educational performance indicated that personality is the most significant factor to predict academic performance. **Fink & McCown (1993)** found that impulsivity seems to be inversely related to academic performance and associated with learning problems consequently, high impulsivity in adolescence showed negative relation of academic performance **(Vigil-Colet & Morales-Vives, 2005)**. **Ferguson, Sanders, O Hehir and James (2000)** found that the personality trait conscientiousness to be a significant predictor of 58% variance upon academic performance.

Panda and Samal (1995) presented a comparative study of personality and academic achievement of adolescent daughters of working and non-working mothers. Result found that working mother's daughters were more extroverted, independent, confident, emotionally stable, aggressive, and less anxious than daughters of non-working mothers.

Tiwari and Poornachand (1995) studied the emotional adjustment among high and low achievers. Result indicated that the high achievers showed significantly high emotional adjustment as compared to low achievers.

Matthews and Deary (1998) found that high conscientiousness persons were associated with personal attributes, learning and academic pursuits, motivated for success and self-control. The openness to experience and conscientiousness is the important predictor of academic performance. Personality characteristics of students are predictors of academic performance **(Busato, Prins, Elshout &Hamaker 1999).**

Rindermann and Neubauer (2001) investigated the influence of personality in different aspect of cognitive performance such as processing speed, intelligence and school performance. Stepwise regression results showed that the weak association of personality and processing speed, average association with intelligence and a highly correlated with academic grades.

Diseth (2003) investigated the association between personality, learning approaches, and academic achievement. Results revealed that the personality factors of openness, neuroticism, and conscientiousness significantly correlated with learning approaches, on the other hand, findings revealed that surface approach negatively correlated with achievement. Neuroticism, openness, and deep approach positively correlated with academic performance, and agreeableness negatively correlated with academic performance.

Chamorro-Premuzic and Furnham (2003) examined the relationship of personality traits and examination performance. Results indicated that the neuroticism significantly correlated with overall academic performance and extraversion only correlated with first year examination, agreeableness and openness to experiences not significantly related with academic performance. The trait conscientiousness positively related with academic performance.

Komarraju and Karau (2005) indicated that conscientiousness and openness are the most significant predictor of academic performance, the result also indicated that motivation plays a mediating role between personality and academic success.

Laidra, Pullman and Allik (2006) investigated that the predicting effect of intelligence and personality on academic performance in college students. Result found that intelligence and personality to be a significant predictor of student's performance. Personality trait neuroticism negatively correlated and agreeableness, openness and conscientiousness positively associated to academic performance. Extraversion trait showed no significant relation with academic performance.

O'Connor and Paunonen (2007) studied the predicting effect of ability intelligent and personality on academic performance. Result found that ability and intelligence as significant predictors of academic achievement and personality play a most significant role of academic performance. **Wagerman and Funder (2007)** found that the factor conscientiousness is a predictor of college performance. The role of openness to experience has been found to be a most important personality factor that predicts academic success **(Komarraju, Karau, & Schmeck, 2009; Laidra et. al., 2007).**

Wright (2008) investigated that the relationship of big five personality traits with academic performance. Correlation results indicated that openness, agreeableness, conscientiousness and emotional stability are positively related to academic performance.

Furnham et al. (2009) found that agreeableness, conscientiousness and extraversion showed asignificance relation on academic performance. The personality trait impulsivity has been most consistently related to academic achievement **(Romano, Babchishin, Pagani & Kohen, 2010; Valiente, Eisenberg, Spinrad, Haugen, Thompson & Kupfer, 2013; Vigil-Colet & Morales-Vives, 2005).**

Eisenberg, Spinrad and Eggum (2010) revealed that impulsive students are more likely to participate in behaviours without enough reflection, engaging in performance that may create direct indulgence at the expense of future achievement.

Viari, Rad and Torabi (2011) studied the personality relation with academic motivation and performance among college students. Findings suggested that academic motivation showed mediation relationship between openness to experience and conscientiousness with academic success.

Camps and Morales-Vives (2013) examined the relation between psychological maturity and personality on adolescent academic achievement performance, results indicated that intelligence and impulsivity were significant predictors of academic success.

Self

Polleys (2001) investigated the relationship of self-regulated learning, personality, and academic achievement. Regression results found a significant relationship between self-regulated learning and personality. The multivariate test found no significant relation between achievement and self-regulated learning.

Van Laar (2000) studied the association of self-esteem with academic success among American and African students. Result found no significant relationship between self-esteem and academic success of American and African students. The academic performance of the students positively correlated with self-esteem **(Bankston & Zhou, 2002; Lockett & Harrell, 2003; Schmidt & Padilla, 2003).**

Reasoner (2005) studied the significance of self-esteem upon academic performance. Result found a close relationship between self-esteem and academic performance. **Lampert (2007)** studied the relationship of self-concept, self-efficacy and academic performance among college students. Result indicated that self-concept and self-efficacy as a significant predictor of college GPA.

Hemalatha (2008) examined the relationship of self-confidence, human relation and academic performance. Results revealed that the self-confidence positively correlated with academic performance. **Naderi, Abdullah, Aizan, Sharir and Kumar (2009)** examined the relationship between self-esteem gender and academic performance. Results revealed that the self-esteem significantly related with academic performance, when gender is controlled there is no significant relationship between self-esteem and student's academic performance.

Gerardi (2005) examined the predicting effect of ability and self-concept on academic performance in technical students. Result indicated that self-concept and ability are a strong predictor of college success. **Yahay, Ramli, Boon, Abd Ghaffar and Zakariya (2009)** examined the association of self-concept, personality with academic performance. Result indicated that self-concept and personality are not significantly correlated with academic performance.

Chetri (2014) studied the relationship between self-concept, achievement motivation and academic performance of adolescent's students. Findings suggested that the significant relationship of self-concept and achievement motivation with academic performance. **Adebule (2014)** studied the self-concept and academic performance in mathematics achievement. Results indicated that the self-concept showed no significant effect on academic performance.

Jerylene and Relton (2014) investigated the relationship between self-esteem and academic performance of college students. Research findings revealed a significant high correlation between academic performance and self-esteem.

Study Habit

In the field of educational research, many studies found a positive relation between the academic performance and study habit **(Onwuegbuzie,**

Slate & Schwartz, 2001). Blumner and Richards (1997) studied the relationship of study habits with academic performance of engineering students. Results revealed a significant relation between study habits and academic performance and no significant gender difference between aptitude or academic grades.

Nandita and Tanima (2004) examined the relationship between study habit and attitude towards studies with academic performance. The result found that attitude towards studies positively correlated with academic performance and also findings suggested that attitude towards studies positively correlated with study habits.

Novhi (2008) examined study habit and skills and academic achievement of medical students and result found a significant correlation between study skill and academic performance. **Nuthana and Yenagi (2009)** examined the relationship between study habit and self-concept with the performance and result found a significant association with academic performance.

Fazal, Hussain, Majaka and Massood (2012) examined the role of study skill in academic performance and result found a significant relationship of study skill and academic performance.

Oluwatimilehin and Owoyele (2012) investigated the relationship of study habits with student's academic success. Results revealed that the study habits and its sub-scales such as "time allocation exercise, concentration, note taking reading and assignments" not a very important factor to affect student's academic performance.

Saini (2013) examined the relationship between study habit, home environment, school environment and academic success of scheduled caste secondary school students and result found a significant association of study habit with academic success. Home environment also plays a significant role in academic success and that school environment does not play a significant role in academic success.

Socio-Demographic Factors – Socio-demographic variables are a more reliable determinant of academic performance. Social factors such as family environment, school environment, socio-economic status of family, parent's education and peer groups widely influences the student's academic performance and also academic performance affected by demographic factors like gender differences, locality, etc. These variables along with some other variables are discussed below:

Family Environment

Parental involvement is the most important part in the development of a child's social and cognitive ability **(Boumrind, 1991)** and the student living in a depressive home environment have lack of socialization and low level of cognitive performance **(Dukes, Payne, Mary & Taylor, 1993).**

Steinberg and Darling (1994) studied how parents and friends influence an youngster's educational performance and how long term plan support from family and friends have been found to influence the student's performance.

Steinberg (1996) and Patten (2000) concluded how parental involvement like homework checking, monitoring the academic involvement in home increases the performance. Parents who communicate their evaluation of academic activities thought of their child encourage education (Musun-Miller & Blevins-Knabe, 1998).

Desimore (1999) investigated the association of parental involvement with student's performance and the findings revealed a significant difference between the parent involvement, race, family income and student's performance. Parent's behaviour, joint family activities influences the child's academic behaviour and motivation **(Grolnick & Slowiaczek, 1994; Heiss, 1996; De Garmo, Forgatch & Martinez, 1999 & Bradley et al., 2000)** and the authoritative parenting style affect positively the student's approach and the difficulty they face in schools **(Gutman & Eccles, 1999 & Bradley et al., 2000).**

Wild, Hofer and Pekrun (2001) concluded that the authoritative parenting style provides the environment conductive to self-regulated learning. The style of parenting not only directly affects the student's attitude, viewpoint and performance. **Van Voorhis (2003)** concluded that the parental involvement influences the performance and is also affected by the family background.

Gartia (2012) examined the association of family environment and academic performance of undergraduate college students. Findings indicated a significant correlation between academic performance and family environment. Students who are in a positive family environment performed better as compared to student's who come from negative family environment.

Gender

Gender is a biogenic factor giving scope for identifiable differences due to the anatomy and physiology of male and female sex. Gender difference plays a vital role in all the affairs of human behaviour and so does in respect of their performance. Many researches show the evidence of the growing gender differences in academic performance **(Fergusson & Horwood 1997; Thiessen & Nickerson, 1999; Praat, 1999; Hillman & Rothman, 2003; Weaver-Hightower, 2003).**

Preece (1999) studied the gender effect of science performance and results indicated that the boys performed better than the girls in the science subject especially in the subject of physics. Another findings show the same results that boys score high in physics as compared to girls and score low in biology than the girls **(Shepardson & Pizzini, 1994 & Heller & Zielger, 1996; Wang & Staver, 1997).**

Hyde, Fennema and Lemon (1990); Spelke (2005) and Hyde and Linn (2006) found that males have usually not performed better than females in science and mathematics. The overall performance of the female student show better than the male students **(Mirza & Mallik, 2000; Rana, 2002) and Rana (2002)** also found that the science performance of girls is better than the science performance of boys.

Numerous studies have reported no individual difference in the cognitive, affective and psychomotor skill achievements of students in reverence of gender **(David & Stanley, 2000; Freedman, 2002; Sungur & Tekkaya, 2003; Arigbabu & Mji, 2004; Din, Ming & Esther, 2004 & Bilesanmi-Awaderu, 2006).**

Samuel and John (2004) studied cooperative class experiment teaching methods effect on student's performance and result found no significant difference in gender achievement between the experimental and control groups but the girls had a little higher mean than the boys.

Kolawole (2007) found that the boys performed better than girls in both competitive and cooperative learning and overall result indicated that the male students performed better than female students in the case of cognitive affective and psychomotor skills of academic performance. **Aguele and Uhumniah (2008)** found that female students achieved lower score than male students in science education. Amitava, Manojit, **Saswata and Braja (2010)** studied the factors affecting a student's academic performance. Result indicated that the boys showed better result than the girls.

Gupta, Sharma and Gupta (2012) examined the role of gender on academic performance in adolescent students and result found no significant difference between boys and girls. **Oludipe (2012)** examined the gender difference on academic performance in the basic science and result found no significant difference of male and female students on academic performance.

Verma (2012) studied the effect of gender, locale and cast on academic performance of students. Findings suggested that the gender have a significant impact on academic performance and most significant findings in mathematics achievement. The boys showed higher academic success as compared to girls.

Locale

Locale is a demographical variable considered under the category of social variable. People are mostly divided into two different groups i.e., rural and urban depending on the density of human created structure and resident people in a particular area. **Fan and Chen (1999)** studied the academic performance among rural and urban area students and result found that rural students do not suffer difficulty only because of their residence in rural areas and their attendance at rural school. **Blackwell and McLaughlin (1999)** found that locality is a significant variable to explain performance and that rural area students attend school generally less than urban area students.

Crowly (2001) found that the rural students academic performance to be less as compared to urban students. The performance of the individuals from urban area was better than the performance of rural area **(Nagaraju, Sumalatha & Reddy, 2003). Owoeye (2002); Howley (2002) and Wobmann (2012)** reported no significant difference between rural and urban area student's academic performance.

Usha (2007) and Singh (2007) found that urban students were superior in academic performance than the rural area students. Another study indicated the same findings i.e., performance of the pupils from urban area to be better than the performance of the rural area **(Ksheersagar, 2008).**

Joshi and Srivastava (2009) found that academic performance of the pupils from urban area was better than the rural area. It was also found that urban area children to be superior in intelligence than the rural area children **(Dhanda & Singh, 2009). Elizabeth (2009)** found a significant difference in academic performance of the urban and rural area student showed higher academic performance than the urban area students.

Verma (2012) examined the impact of gender, locale and cast on academic performance of students. Result indicated that the locale significantly affected the academic performance. The urban area students reported high level of academic performance as compare to rural area students and **Alokan et al. (2013)** studied the difference between rural and urban area student's academic performance and result revealed no significant difference in performance of the student's of rural area.

Parental Education

Many factors influence a student's ability and achievement, but parental education is one of the most significant predictor of child academic performance **(Haveman & Wolfe, 1995; Klebanav, Books-Gunn & Dunkan, 1994; Smith, Books-Gunn & Klebanav, 1999).** The education level of parents is a strong predictor of student's academic success. Parents' education influences the cognitive competence, opportunities for the education, and value and utility of education. These factors affect the student's educational motivation and they achieve better in the educational field. **(Blok & Saris, 2000; Erickson & Jonson, 1996; Ferguson & Woodward, 2000).**

Bhatnagar and Sharma (1992) studied the association among parent's education and student's academic performance. Results indicated that the parents who attend school and perform better academically influence their children's academic performance. It's clear that the education of parents is significantly connected to academic performance of the students.

Eccles (1993) found that parent's behavior lead to positive outcomes for the children and youth. Parent's education level is a significant predictor of parental involvement in their child's schooling and success **(Keith et al, 1998; Shumow & Miller, 2001).**

Smith Brooks Gunn and Klebandv (1997) found the association of family income and parent education with children's academic performance affected by the home environment. Parent's education directly affected their child's academic performance **(Jimerson, Egeland & Teo, 1999).**

Campbell, Hombo and Mazzeo (1999) found that the students who reported the highest level of parent education tended to higher levels of educational outcomes. The parent's who had a high level of education have superior expectation for their children's education as compared to parent's who have low levels of education **(Singh et al., 1995; Gill & Reynolds, 1999).**

Crowyn and Bradley (2002) found that maternal education directly affected children's cognitive and behavioural outcomes.

Englund, Uckner, Whaley and Egeland (2004) concluded that the highly educated mothers provided more positive support for their child's education and problem solving and result also revealed that mothers provide suitable arrangements for the study and coordinate the child's behaviours and activities in childhood had a higher level of intelligence. The intelligent showed positive relation with performance and high academic performance early in school contribute to better performance in later age. **Pamela and Kean (2005)** found that parent's education in their children's learning influences the academic performance of their academic performance.

Sharma and Jha (2014) studied the effect of parental education, institute and gender on academic performance. Result indicated that the parent's education play a significant role in academic performance. Highly educated parents child showed good academic performance as compared to less educated parent's child. Gender and type of institution also significantly affect the student's performance.

Peer Group

Peer groups of individuals are positively and negatively related with performance. The peer groups are the role model of the students and the positive role model help to improve academic performance and the negative role model give unpleasant outcomes **(Lockwood & Kunda, 2002)**. Several study indicated a significant relation of peer groups quality with academic performance (**Betts & Morell, 1999; Epple & Romano, 1998; Hanushek, Kain, Markman & Rivkin, 2003; Sawkins, 2002)**.

Vandenberghe (2002); Zimmer and Toma (2000); Zimmerman (2003) examined the relation between peer quality and academic performance. Result indicated that a better quality of peer group influences the statistically and economically performance, also, they affect a student's academic performance. **Paola and Scoppa (2010)** study reported that the positive peer group affect the ability of performance.

Misanya and Sophy (2013) studied the peer influence on academic performance on boarding school girls; the findings suggested that student's great score had a positive influence of the academic performance. **Bonin (2013)** examined the effect of peer mentors on academic performance. Findings suggested that the effect of peer mentors positively influence the social and academic performance.

Korir and Kipkembai (2014) studied the influence of school environment and peer effect on a student's academic success. Result indicated that the school environment positively affects students' performance and also the peer level has a strong relation with student's academic performance. Students peer group involved in negative activities i.e., sneaking, drugs, out of school, influence the student's academic performance. **Robert (2014)** studied the relation between academic performance and peer effects of students. Result revealed that the peer effect is the most significant factor to influence the academic performance of students.

Socio-Economic Status

Socio-economic status is measured as a grouping factor, including family income, occupation and education level. **Byrne and Byrne (1990)** stated that the parent's socio-economic status is concerned to children's academic performance. Socio-economic is one of the contributing factors of a student's academic performance **(Smith, 1993). Velez, Schiefelbein and Valenzuella (1993)** studied the relationship among family background and student's performance and the findings show that socio-economic status is positively associated with a student's academic performance. Higher socio-economic status of parents increases their children's academic outcomes **(Argyle, 1994).**

Harrish, Brady and Herman (1996) concluded that family income plays a significant role on children's academic performance and development. Student's with a higher level of socio-economic status had higher levels of academic success as compared to students who have lower level of socio-economic status and result also indicated a statistically significant difference between socio-economic status and academic performance **(Kruse, 1996).**

Saito (1999) studied the effect of socio-economic status and educational performance and the findings suggested that socio-economic status was not related to academic performance. A student's family income influences their academic outcome in adolescent stage **(Rhea & Otto, 2001).**

McMillan and Westor (2002) concluded that the socio-economic status was responsible for the student's performance in the context of parent education, occupation and income. **Considine and Zappala (2002)** studied the effect of socio-economic difficulty in the academic performance of school students and findings revealed that parents who are strong educationally, socially and economically encourage the academic performance in their children.

Escarce (2003) found the educational facilities available by the parents of adolescents educational performance. Students who come from lower socio-economic background perform poorly in academic examination as compared to students who come from higher socio-economic background **(Jeynes, 2002; Hansen & Mastekaasa, 2003; Eamon, 2005).**

Jacob and Harvey (2005) found that the students from lower income group and single parent homes performed better and many students from higher income group performed badly in academics. **Casanova et al. (2005)** examined the influences of family and social demographic variables on student's performance and result found that social, demographic variable a better predictor of performance and family variable played an important role in academic performance.

Marks, Cresswell and Ainley (2006) studied the relationship between socio-economic status on a fifteen year old student's performance in a different culture. The result indicated that culture played a very important role in student's performance and socio-economic status showed stronger relation with academic performance.

Benilton, Cibele, Norberto, Perosa and Rafael (2006) studied the effect of educational and socio-economic conditions of parent's on academic performance and result indicated students who come from lower socio-economic and educational background performed better as compared to students who come from higher socio-economic and educational background.

Farooq, Chaudhury, Shafiq and Berhanu (2011) indicated that socio-economic status and parent's education significantly influenced the student's academic performance. The high and average socio-economic level influences the performance more than low level.

Suleman et al. (2012) studied the effect of socio-economic status on the academic performance of secondary school students and result found that parental socio-economic status and education, occupation and income level influences the academic performance of students.

Ogunshola and Adewale (2012) studied the influence of socio-economic status on academic performance, and results revealed that the parental education and socio-economic status do not significantly influence the academic performance.

Kumar (2013) examined the association of socio-economic status with academic performance of adolescent students. Results indicated that the socio-economic status positively related with academic performance of both male/female and rural/urban students.

School Environment

The learning atmosphere as the psychological and sociological circumstance or determinant of performance (Fraser, 1994), classroom environment is the most important factor of a student's performance. **Diekhoe and Wigginton (1992)** studied that college faculty perception of classroom environment and classroom environment is related to self-perception and reflect the learning performance.

Cheng (1994) examines the relationship between a student's affective performance and classroom environment and result found a positive environment is highly correlated with a student's affective performance. **Dorman (1997)** studied the relationship between the classroom environment and school performance and result found a weak relationship between school performance and classroom environment.

Freiberg (1998) found that the school climate positively influences the health of the learning environment. Classroom atmosphere significantly affected a student's performance; a positive school environment enhances the performance **(Masutha & Ackermann, 1999).**

Kim (2000) studied the association of classroom environment and academic success. Result found a positive relationship of classroom environment and student outcome attitude. **Beak and Choi (2002)** examined the relationship between classroom environment student's perception and academic performance and result found that student perception in a classroom had a significant correlation with academic performance.

Goh and Khine (2002) findings showed that a good student-teacher relationship is better to form and maintain a positive classroom climate and increase the performance. Student perception of teacher support related to a greater feeling of school belonging and engagement and motivation as well as better academic performance **(Ma, 2003).**

Suzanna (2003) found that students who actively participated in classroom perform better as compared to students who do not participate in a classroom. **Eshel and Kohavi (2003)** studied that perceived classroom control, learning strategy, self-regulation with academic performance and findings suggested a significant association among classroom control and academic performance.

Jayshree and Chrisenduth (2006) investigated the influence of classroom environment on academic performance and result found a significant association between the classroom environment and academic performance. **Talton and Simpson (2006)** examined the relationship of classroom climate to attitude towards science achievement and result revealed that student attitude towards the classroom climate predicted the science achievement.

Fraser (2007) indicated that classroom learning environment, a statistically significant factor of academic achievement score. Constructive learning environment variable and motivational beliefs variables were positively associated with performance **(Nazmiya & Arisoy, 2007).**

Lau and Lee (2008) examined the relation between academic goal and their relation to students perceived classroom environment and result found that student perception of classroom environment was significantly associated with personal achievement goals.

Sungur (2009) examined the relationship between classroom climate, self-regulation and science performance. The result found that classroom climate positively associated with motivation and cognitive component of self-regulation and science performance. The classroom environment increased the academic performance and decreased the disturbing behaviour **(Guaedino & Fullerton, 2010).**

Garland (2010) studied the relation among student involvement and academic performance in higher education and result revealed a significant association among performance. **Chiaki and Konishi (2010)** studied the student-teacher relation and academic performance and findings suggested that a positive student-teacher relationship is related to better academic performance.

The students who perceived positive classroom environment achieve high score in schools than the students who perceived negative classroom environment **(Okonkwo, 2010; Okoh, 2011) and Wei and Elias (2011)** also found that students perception in their classroom environment, having affiliation were extrinsically motivated and results also revealed that student affiliation and task orientation in classroom were positively correlated with their motivation and involvement showed the negative relationship.

Chapter Three

ISSUE AND PROPOSED ASSUMPTIONS

The main aim of this chapter is to formulate the problems and hypotheses of the present research work undertaken. The proper selecting and defining research problem is the most important step of any research process. Though posing a problem, it is to be kept in mind that the problems allow you to generate many different empirically testable questions.

Objectives

- To examine the effect of personality factor separately on the academic performance.
- To examine the effect of morningness-eveningness preference on the academic performance.
- To examine the effect of gender on the academic performance.

Education is one of the most important part of developing individuals' and playing an essential role in the development of the nation. Better education qualities contribute and have a great impact on the development of the country and their economic, social and political system. Here the academic performance of students' significantly affects the growth of the country. Academic performance is the outcome of education; and indicate the degrees of students' academic goals. In this competitive world, academic performance of the students is an indicator of their future. In all cultures, the performance of the students is the essential goal of the educational process. A students' academic performance explains the excelling in their institutions, if they performed excellent or good in their academy they will be ensured a successful livelihood. For this the personality of the students' plays a significant role and influence a students' academic performance. Several research findings indicated that personality factors predict the academic performance and its emphasis to improving their performance on the institutions. Although a large amount of studies consistently have shown evidence of the relationship between academic performance of the students' and different aspects of the personality **(Allik, 2007; Busato, Elshout, Hamaker, Prins, 1999; Chowdhury, 2006; De Fruyt & Mervielde, 1996; Furnham & Chamorro-Premuzic, 2003; Komarraju, Korea, & Schmeck, 2009; Laidra et. al., 2007; Laidra, Pullmann, & Duff, 2004; Neubauer & Rindermann 2001; O'Connor & Paunonen 2007; Rogers, 2005; Trapmann Hell, Hirn & Schuler 2007).** These studies stated that the personality variables explain the prediction of academic performance. **Furnham and Chamorro-Premuzic (2006)** reported that the relationship with academic performance and personality would reflect equivalent correlations of intelligence with personality. Healthy personality developed one of the most necessary goals of education and also helps educators to improve the performance of the students on the structure of their personality **(Kuppuswamy, 2000)**. A present study also studied the role of morningness-eveningness preference on academic performance of the students'. The learning time preference is the most important factor to influence the academic performance. Morningness-eveningness preference is able to explain the variation in the expression of biological and behavioral patterns being a 'morning type' or 'evening type' and 'intermediate type' is a stable characteristic. Most of the findings demonstrate that the adult student shows better performance in the morning than later in the day and evening time show worse performance than the morning and afternoon time **(Besoluk, 2010; Goldstein, Hasher, Hahn, Wiprzycha and Zelazo, 2006; Goldstein, Hasher & May, 2005; May, 1999).** The gender of the student also has a influence on their academic performance. Gender difference plays a vital role in all the relationships of human behaviour and so does in respect of their performance. Therefore, the present study has been undertaken to observate and to examine the impact of personality, morningness-eveningness preference and gender on academic performance and the problem and their related hypothesis of the present research work is as under:

Personality and Academic Performance

Numerous studies show the evidence of the association of personality with academic performance of the students' **(Allik, 2007; Busato, Prins, Elshout & Hamaker 1999; Furnham & Chamorro-Premuzic, 2003; Chowdhury, 2006; De Fruyt & Mervielde, 1996; Komarraju, Karau, & Schmeck, 2009; Laidra, Pullmann, & Duff, 2004; Neubauer & Rindermann, 2001; O'Connor & Paunonen 2007; Rothstein Paunonen, Rush & King, 1994).**

1. The first problem of the present work is to examine whether the subject showing low neuroticism differ significantly in their academic performance than the subjects showing high neuroticism.

Neuroticism correlated with study attitudes of school children and university students (**Crede & Kuncel, 2008; Heaven, Mak, Barry & Ciarrochi, 2002; Busato, Prins, Elshout, & Hamaker, 2000).** Neuroticism shows the negative relation with academic performance **(Hakimi et al., 2011; Trapmann Hell, Hirn and Schuler, 2007).** Neuroticism correlated with academic achievement, particularly for the factor of impulsivity and anxiety. **(Kuncel et al., 2005; O'Connor & Paunonen, 2007).** The trait impulsivity has been most consistently related to academic achievement **(Romano, Babchishin, Pagani & Kohen, 2010; Valiente, Eisenberg, Spinrad, Haugen, Thompson & Kupfer, 2013; Vigil-Colet & Morales-Vives, 2005). Fink & McCown (1993)** found that impulsivity is inversely related with academic performance and associated with learning problems consequently; high impulsivity in adolescence is showing negative relation of academic performance. **Wright (2008)** indicated that emotional stability is positively related to academic performance. Emotional stability is associated with performance **(Judge & Bono, 2002; Robbins et al., 2004)**. Neuroticism is significantly and negatively related with academic performance. **(Chamorro-Premuzic & Furnham, 2003; Laidra, Pullman & Allik, 2006; Lathey, 1991; Rogers, 2005; Sanchez-Marin et al., 2001).**

Taking this evidence into consideration the present study would test the hypothesis that the subjects with low neuroticism would show higher academic performance than the subjects with high neuroticism.

2. The second problem of the present work is to examine whether the subjects who show low extraversion differ significantly in their academic performance than the subjects showing high extraversion.

Extraversion was a successful predictor of school performance **(Lievens, Cortsier, Defruyt & DeMaessneer, 2002; Schniederjan et al., 2005)**. Some studies show that the extravert performed better in the oral examination and introvert has benefits to written examinations **(Chamorro-premuzic & Furnham, 2003; Furnham & Medhurst, 1995; Robinson, Gabriel, & Katchan, 1993). Furnham et al. (2009)** found that the extraversion shows the significance relation on academic performance. A small amount of the studies indicated that the personality trait extraversion is positively related to academic performance **(Busto et al, 1999; Chowdhury, 2006; Eysenck 1992; Dietz, Felder & Felder, 2002; Salehi, Khak & Alam, 2013; Shokri, Kadivar, Naghsh, Daneshvarpour & Molaei, 2007). De Raad and Schouwenburg (1996)** reported that those students who have highly extravert will perform better academically.

Taking this evidence into consideration the present study would test the hypothesis that the subjects with low extraversion would show low academic performance than the subjects with high extraversion.

3. The third problem of the present work is to examine whether the subjects who show low openness differ significantly in their academic performance than the subjects showing high openness.

The role of openness is the most important personality factor that predicts academic performance **(Busato, Prins, Elshout & Hamaker 1999; Komarraju & Karau, 2005; Komarraju, Karau, & Schmeck, 2009; Laidra et. al., 2007; Viari, Rad &Torabi, 2011)**. Openness also seems to be positively related to academic performance **(Geisler-Brenstein & Schmeck, 1996; Komarraju, Karau & Schmeck, 2009; Melissa, O'Connor & Sampo, 2007)**. Openness is also related to better scores in vocabulary and general knowledge **(Ackerman & Heggestad, 1997; Ashton, Lee, Vernon, & Jang, 2000; Goff & Ackerman, 1992).**

Openness is positively linked with learning approaches **(Vermetten, et al., 2001) Farsides & Woodfield (2003)** indicated that openness has been positively associated with grade point. Openness is positively associated with academic performance **(Chowdhury, 2006; Farsides & Woodfield, 2003; Gray & Watson, 2002; Lievens et al., 2002 McKenzie & Gow, 2004; Phillips et al., 2003; Rogers, 2005; Rothstein, Paunonen, Rush & King, 1994; Wright, 2008).**

Taking this evidence into consideration the present study would test the hypothesis that the subjects with low openness would show low academic performance than the subjects with high openness.

4. The fourth problem of the present work is to examine whether the subjects who show low agreeableness differ significantly in their academic performance than the subjects showing high agreeableness.

Agreeableness is usually not associated with academic performance of students yet some studied related to this personality trait suggested a positive relation with agreeableness and academic performance **(De Raad & Schouwenburg; Rogers, 2005; McKenzie and Gow 2004; Wright, 2008). Furnham et al. (2009)** found that agreeableness shows a significance relation on academic performance. Agreeableness shows a significant positive relation with academic performance. **(Farsides & Woodfield, 2003; Gray & Watson, 2002; Rothstein Paunonen, Rush & King, 1994).**

Taking this evidence into consideration the present study would test that the subjects with low agreeableness would show low academic performance than the subjects with high agreeableness.

5. The fifth problem of the present work is to examine whether the subjects who show low conscientiousness differ significantly in their academic performance than the subjects showing high conscientiousness.

The trait, Conscientiousness is clearly related to academic performance **(Heaven & Ciarrochi, 2012; Rosander, Bcakstrom & Stenberg, 2011). Wagerman and Funder (2007)** found that the factor conscientiousness is a predictor of academic performance **(Busato, Prins, Elshout &Hamaker 1999; Furnham et al., 2009; Laidra, Pullmann, & Allik, 2007; Shiner, R. L., & Masten, A. S., 2002; Noftle & Robins, 2007; Viari, Rad, Torabi, 2011). Duff et al., (2004)** research shows that conscientiousness is a significant predictor of academic performance in university students. Ferguson, Sanders, **O Hehir and James (2000)** found that the personality trait conscientiousness has a significant variance upon academic performance **(Lievens, Cortsier, Defruyt & DeMaessneer, 2002). Wright (2008)** indicated that conscientiousness is positively related to academic performance and also **Chowdhury (2006); Rogers (2005); McKenzie and Gow (2004)** reported that the personality factor conscientiousness is positively connected with a student's academic success **(Busato et al., 2000; Furnham & Chamorro-Premuzic 2003; Conard, 2006; Kling, 2001; Salgado, 1997).**

Taking this evidence into consideration the present study would test the hypothesis that the subjects with low conscientiousness would show low academic performance than the subjects with high conscientiousness.

Gender and Academic Performance

6. The sixth problem of the present work is to investigate the role of sex in academic performance.

A lot of studies indicate that gender also influence academic performance. Many researches show the evidence of the growing gender differences in academic performance **(Fergusson & Horwood 1997; Thiessen & Nickerson, 1999; Praat, 1999; Hillman & Rothman, 2003; Weaver-Hightower, 2003). Hyde, Fennema and Lemon (1990); Spelke (2005); Hyde and Linn (2006) f**ound that males normally did not preform better than females in science and mathematics. The overall performance of the female student show better than the male students **(Mirza & Mallik, 2000; Rana, 2002) and Rana (2002)** also found that the science performance of girls is better than the science performance of the boys. **Amitava, Maojit, Saawata and Braja (2010)** found that the students gender influence their academic performance and they also reveal that the boys perform poorly as compared to girls. Boys are more underachieving students than girls **(McCall, 1994).** Females show better performance than males **(Escribano, Iaz-Morales, Delgdo & Collado, 2011; Mirza & Malik, 2000; Rana, 2000).**

Considering the evidence of the above discussion the present study would test the hypothesis that the female subjects would show higher academic performance than the male subjects.

Morningness-Eveningness Preference and Academic Performance

7. The seventh and the last problem of the present work is to examine whether or not the subject of different morningness-eveningness preference would differ significantly in their academic performance.

Humans are normally active in daytime as compared to afternoon and evening time. Morningness–Eveningness preference that is morning active type or evening active type or intermediate type persons (Circadian typology) has been found to be capable of explaining the variation in the expression of biological and behavioural patterns. Most of the findings demonstrate that an adult student shows better performance in the morning than later in the day and evening time show bad performance than the morning and afternoon time **(Hasher, Goldstein & May, 2005; Itons-Peterson, Rocchi, West, McLellan & Hackney, 1998; May, 1999). Goldstein, Hahn, Hasher, Wiprzycha and Zelazo (2006)** found that evening type adolescents show poor academic performance. Morning type students performed better than evening type students **(Besoluk, 2010; Beşoluk, Onder & Deveci, 2011; Randal & Frech, 2009). Preckel, Lipnevich, Schneider and Roberts (2011)** found that eveningness negatively associated with academic succes. The morningness shows a positive relationship with academic performance **(Franzisp, Anastasiya, Sandra & Richard, 2011).**

Considering the evidence of the above discussion the present study would test the hypothesis that the subjects with morning preference would show better academic performance as compared to the subjects with evening preference. The subjects with intermediate preference would remain in between the above two.

Chapter Four

APPROACH OR RESEARCH METHODOLOGY

The method and research design can be termed as a spine of the whole research process. The method helps the investigator to make a scientific investigation in a more easy way. Through research we can look for new facts in any branch of knowledge. The validity and dependability of any research work are judged on the basis of the soundness and scientificness of its methodology. The accurate methodology plays a very important role in implementing the research work scientifically. Research methodology constitutes a significant aspect of any scientific investigation and the dependability of its finding depends upon the extent to which the researchers have incorporated, sophisticated research methodology which includes the sampling technique employed, the tools used, the research design operated and procedures followed.

Design

The present study is a research employing type- S independent variables. The purpose of the study investigates the effect of personality, morningness-eveningness preference and gender on academic performance. For this purpose a 2x2x3 factorial design was computed to analyze the data in which each personality dimensions (high & low scorers), gender (male & female) and morningness-eveningness preference (morning type, intermediate type & evening type) was considered as independent variables. The overall marks obtained by the students were taken as the dependent variable.

The subjects were divided into two subgroups of personality dimension on the basis of quartile Q1-Q3 range. The subject scoring high from the Q3 and the subject scoring low from the Q1 (excluding the subjects falling the semi-interquartile range) were considered as the subjects of high and low score of personality dimension respectively, Therefore, the number of subjects declining in each cell was not equal. Since the personality has five dimensions so, each personality dimension would be taken separately with morningness-eveningness preference and gender. In this way 2 each personality dimension separately (high & low) x 2 gender (male & female) x 3 morningness-eveningness preference (morning type, intermediate type & evening active) design was obtained.

Factor – A - factor a is the five Personality dimension, each dimension has two levels (a1, a2)

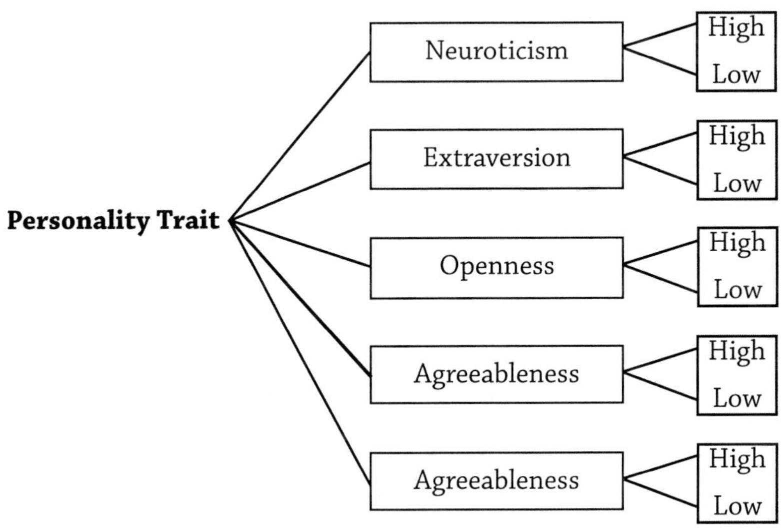

Factor – B - factor b is the Gender; it has two levels (b1, b2)

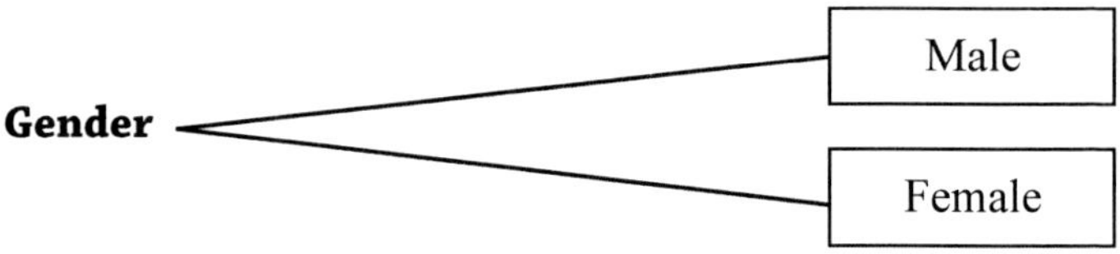

Factor – C - factor c is the Morningness-Eveningness Preference, it has three levels (c1, c2, c3)

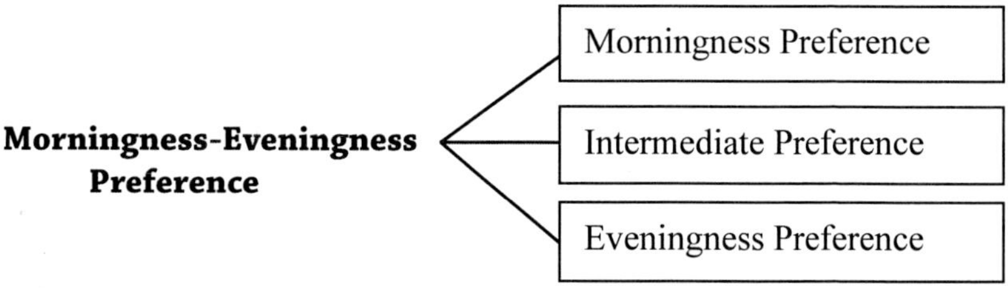

Treatment Combination – **2x2x3** factorial design

p Levels of (A) where p= 2 (a1, a2)

q Levels of (B) where q= 2 (b1, b2)

r Levels of (C) where r= 3 (c1, c2, c3)

Table – 4.1

Block Diagram of pqr (2x2x3) factorial design

Groups	a_1		a_2	
	b_1	b_2	b_1	b_2
c_1	$a_1 b_1 c_1$	$a_1 b_2 c_1$	$a_2 b_1 c_1$	$a_2 b_2 c_1$
c_2	$a_1 b_1 c_2$	$a_1 b_2 c_2$	$a_2 b_1 c_2$	$a_2 b_2 c_2$
c_3	$a_1 b_1 c_3$	$a_1 b_2 c_3$	$a_2 b_1 c_3$	$a_2 b_2 c$

The total number of treatment = 12 used for each personality factor.

This design will be capable to discover the main effect of (1) Personality, (2) Gender and (3) Morningness-Eveningness Preference for academic performance. The interaction effect of personality **x** gender; gender **x** morningness-eveningness preference; personality **x** morningness-eveningness preference has also been examined as well as the second order interaction effect between personality x gender x morningness-eveningness will be ascertained with the help of this design.

Sample

In the present work a stratified random sampling technique was used. The total number of 1108 students was taken in which 626 were male (56.49%) students and 482 (43.50%) were female students respectively. The subjects were selected from different engineering colleges situated in Raipur and Durg district of Chhattisgarh state. The age range of the participants was 18-20 years. In the present study, the samples of engineering students were split into a number of categories on the basis of three specific characteristics:

Personality	-	High
		Low
Gender	-	Male
		Female
M-E Preference	-	Morning type
		Intermediate type
		Evening type

This type of stratification is known as complex stratification. Thus, 2x2x3 factorial design have unequal subjects in each cells. A total number of 1108 subjects were randomly drawn following the stratified random sampling technique. The particular of the finally selected sample is shown in table - 2.

Table – 4.2

Particular of the sample

Groups	Neuroticism				Extraversion				Openness				Agreeableness				Conscientiousness			
	High a_1		Low a_2		High a_1		Low a_2		High a_1		Low a_2		High a_1		Low a_2		High a_1		Low a_2	
	M b_1	F b_2	M b_1	F b_2	M b_1	F b_2	M b_1	F b_2	M b_1	F b_2	M b_1	F b_2	M b_1	F b_2	M b_1	F b_2	M b_1	F b_2	M b_1	F b_2
Morning type c_1	(s_1) 61	(s_2) 61	(s_3) 84	(s_4) 53	(s_5) 94	(s_6) 72	(s_7) 59	(s_8) 47	(s_9) 89	(s_{10}) 74	(s_{11}) 66	(s_{12}) 50	(s_{13}) 93	(s_{14}) 76	(s_{15}) 71	(s_{16}) 41	(s_{17}) 95	(s_{18}) 82	(s_{19}) 56	(s_{20}) 15
Intermediate type c_2	(s_{21}) 66 S	(s_{22}) 62	(s_{23}) 77	(s_{24}) 49	(s_{25}) 81	(s_{26}) 64	(s_{27}) 68	(s_{28}) 66	(s_{29}) 70	(s_{30}) 52	(s_{31}) 70	(s_{32}) 74	(s_{33}) 65	(s_{34}) 71	(s_{35}) 94	(s_{36}) 66	(s_{37}) 56	(s_{38}) 54	(s_{39}) 79	(s_{40}) 54
Evening type c_3	(s_{41}) 30	(s_{42}) 25	(s_{43}) 39	(s_{44}) 13	(s_{45}) 37	(s_{46}) 17	(s_{47}) 34	(s_{48}) 28	(s_{49}) 66	(s_{50}) 16	(s_{51}) 33	(s_{52}) 25	(s_{53}) 28	(s_{54}) 13	(s_{55}) 44	(s_{56}) 21	(s_{57}) 14	(s_{58}) 8	(s_{59}) 48	(s_{60}) s25

The cells were different in size and they were considered as acceptable **(Winer, 1971)**

Table-4.3

The frequencies of the subjects on the basis of three independent variables are given in the table as under:

Variables	**groups**	**Frequency**
Gender	Male	626
	Female	482
M- E Preference	Morning Type	467
	Intermediate Type	471
	Evening Type	170

Personality Dimensions (Q1-Q3)

Neuroticism	High	305
	Low	315
Extroversion	High	365
	Low	302
Openness	High	334
	Low	318
Agreeableness	High	346
	Low	337
Conscientiousness	High	309
	Low	277

Measures

Research measures are very necessary in any research because without measures it cannot be significant. Tool in research refers to the scales or measures or questionnaires, used to conduct the present research.

Independent Measures

Personality

To measure personality **NEO Five Factor Inventory** prepared by Costa **and McCrae (1992)** was used. This inventory measures five dimensions of personality, i.e., Neuroticism, Extraversion, Openness, Agreeableness and Conscientiousness. It consisted of 60 items (12 items in each dimension) using a 5-point rating scale ranging from strongly disagree = 1 to strongly agree = 5. The internal consistency coefficient reported in the manual were Neuroticism = .79, Extraversion = .79, Openness = .80, Agreeableness = .75, Conscientiousness = .83 and the validity of the scale is ranging from .75 to .89 correlated with the NEO-PI. The Cronbach's alpha coefficients of the present sample were Neuroticism = .56, Extraversion = .53, Openness = .67, Agreeableness = .53, Conscientiousness = .67 and the overall reliability of the present research work are .73 calculated by the Cronbach's alpha.

The tools used in the present study were given in the appendix.

Personality Dimensions

S. NO.	Personality Dimension	Characteristics
1.	**Neuroticism**	This type of person is anxious, generally apprehensive and prone to worry. They often get angry at others, but has only usual periods of unhappiness that most men experience, embarrassment or shyness when dealing with strangers is often a problem for them. They report being better at controlling their impulses and desires, unable to handle stress well. High scores tend to be more sensitive, nervous, worrying, insecure and depressive and low scores tend to be secure, confident, relaxed and hardy.
2.	**Extraversion**	This type of individual is average in their level of interpersonal warmth, but rarely enjoys large and noisy crowds or parties. They have trouble asserting themselves and prefer to stay in the background in meetings and group discussions. They have moderate level of personal energy and activity level and experience as much joy and happiness as most men. High scorers tend to be outgoing, energetic, fun loving, frank, assertive and sociable and low scores tend to be an introvert, quiet, withdraw, reserved, shy and unsociable

3.	**Openness**	In experiential style, this individual is generally open. They have a vivid imagination and an active fantasy life. They are particularly responsive to beauty as found in music, art, poetry or nature and his feeling and emotional reactions are varied and important to him. They are interested in intellectual challenges and unusual ideas and perspectives and he is generally liberal in his social, political and moral beliefs. High scorers tend to be inventive, curious, broad interests, liberal, unique and complex and low scores tend to be cautious, uncreative, narrow interest, down to earth and traditional
4.	**Agreeableness**	This type of person tends to be cynical, skeptical and suspicious and has a low opinion of human nature. They are very sincere and would find it difficult to deceive or manipulate others and he is reasonably considerate of others and responds to request with others for help. They hold their own in conflicts with others and also willing to forgive and forget. They are hard-headed and tough-minded, and his social and political attitudes reflect his pragmatic realism. High scorers tend to be friendly, compassionate, forgiving, courteous orderly, altruistic, kind, gentle, and humility and low scores tend to be competitive, critical, callous, rude, harsh, self-centeredness, hostility, indifference and unkindness

5.	**Conscientiousness**	This individual is rational, prudent, practical, resourceful and well-prepared. They are very punctual and well-organized and highly conscientious. They have a high level of aspiration and strive for excellence in whatever they do. They are cautious and deliberate and think carefully before acting. High scorers tend to be efficient, organized, careful, self disciplined, orderly, responsible and thorough and low scores tend to be careless, undependable, negligent and disorganized

Morningness-Eveningness Preference

To assess the M-E preference of the subject Morningness-Eveningness Questionnaire **(Horne & Ostberg, 1976)** modified by the School of Life Science, Pt. Ravishankar Shukla University was used. This Questionnaire consists of 7 items. It is based upon a scale score ranging from 5 to 32. The subject will be identified with either Morning type (MT) or Intermediate type (IT) or Evening type (ET), depending upon the total score they achieved between 23-32 (MT), 16-22 (IT) and 5-15 (ET), respectively on the MEQ. In the present study MT, IT and ET type subjects were included.

Dependent Measure

Academic Performance

To assess the academic performance the marks obtained by the engineering students in their previous semester examination i.e., first semester was used. Since selected students were taken from two different examination boards their percentage can't be compared for comparison purpose and obtained marks of each student's were converted into standard scores (T scores), taking the mean (along with standard deviation) of a particular board exam. The average academic performance score of **Chhattisgarh Swami Vivekananda Technical University (CSVTU)** was found 71.618 (SD = 9.751) were as it was 69.834 (SD = 9.751) in the case of the National Institute of Technology (NIT). Taking these mean, SD and T score were calculated with a formula [T = ((X-m)/sd) X 10] + 50. It was done for each subject and obtained T scores were treated as academic performance of the subjects.

Procedure

In the present study the researcher explained the objectives of the research work and permission was obtained from the proper channel and the Director/Principal/HOD of different engineering colleges in Raipur and Drug District of Chhattisgarh State was sent to collect. The researcher collected the students in their institution and established a good rapport with the subjects and they were assured that their responses and their identities will be kept under strict confidence and will not be disclosed anywhere. Thus, they are free to give their answers, comfortably and honestly anything they felt. In this way subjects, were encouraged to give their proper co-operation during the testing. After establishing a good rapport with the subjects' both the measures i.e., personality questionnaire and Morningness-Eveningness Preference scale were administered to them with proper instructions. In this Questionnaire, the item is related to yourself and your activities next to each statement to five alternative answers are written, and the second Questionnaire related to your activeness in day or night time and each statement 4 or 5 alternative answers are written. Please choose the one option which describes your best behaviour, do not leave any question, and reply to all questions.

After giving the instructions to each subject they were asked to give their response on only one option by marking ( ) before every statement. Thus, for all Questionnaire sample responses were obtained, generally each subject took 25-30 minutes to complete the tests. After completion, questionnaire was taken and scores given. The scoring was completed according to the scoring system given by the author of the questionnaires. After scoring, the data were organized and put for the statistical analysis. The data were analyzed with the help of appropriate statistical techniques, in order to verify the formulated hypotheses and the results and discussion are presented in the next chapter.

Chapter Five

OUTCOMES AND INTERPRETATION

The purpose of the present work is to investigate the effect of personality, morningness-eveningness preference and gender on academic performance. To accomplish this goal the subjects of both sexes were taken from the technical institute of engineering from Chhattisgarh state. Five personality factors of the subjects were examined by the **NEO Five Factor Personality Inventory** and to measure the morningness-eveningness preference, Morningness-Eveningness Questionnaire was used. Data were analysed by the three way ANOVAs taking each personality factors (high and low), morningness-eveningness preference (morning type, intermediate type and evening type) gender (male and female) as independent variables. Academic performance scores (percentage of the students result) were considered a dependent variable. Before computing the data through ANOVA statistic, it was necessary to see that the basic assumption of ANOVA should be satisfied. The two basic assumption of ANOVA are given below:

- The first assumption is that the distribution of the dependent variable scores in every treatment population is normal.

- The second assumption is homogeneity of variance, it explains that the variances in the population scores in each of the treatment group must be homogeneous.

The first assumption is satisfied since the samples are randomly selected from population and also because the size of the sample is comparatively large. **Gravetter & Wallnau (1997)** suggested that the first assumption i.e., normality of distribution is satisfied without difficulty and is not a cause for concern in most researches. When there is a reason to suspect that the population are far normal in figure, it may be compensated by ensuring that the samples are relatively large, i.e., around 30 or more, for testing the second assumption i.e., homogeneity of variance is an important one. Therefore in the present research, an attempt has been made to check the nature of group by computing Levene's test of homogeneity of variance. The summary of the Levene's Tests is shown in table -5.1

Table No. – 5.1

Summary of Levene's test for homogeneity of variance for academic performance scores of five ANOVA groups based on different five personality factors, morningness-eveningness preference and gender

S. No.	Personality Factors	F	df1	df2	Sig
1.	Neuroticism	.512	11	608	.896
2.	Extraversion	.940	11	655	.501
3.	Openness	1.677	11	640	.074
4.	Agreeableness	1.342	11	671	.197
5.	Conscientiousness	1.046	11	574	.404

The observed values of Levene's test of homogeneity of variance for five personality factors are found to be not significant which reveal that the data provide evidence that the homogeneity of variance assumption has not been desecrated. The researchers enabled to analyze the data through ANOVA statistics. Thus the three way ANOVAs was used to analyze the data in which, as mentioned previously, each personality factors (high and low scorers), morningness-eveningness preference (morning type, intermediate type and evening type) gender (male and female) were analyzed as independent variables. Academic performance scores (percentage of the students) were considered a dependent variable. In the following, result of each ANOVA shall be discussed separately.

Personality Factor Neuroticism

Table No. -5.2

Average academic performance scores of the groups of personality (Neuroticism), gender and morningnes-eveningness preference

Variables	Groups	Average Scores of Academic Performance
Personality (Neuroticism)	High	69.10 n = 305
	Low	72.31 n = 315
Gender	Male	67.90 n = 357
	Fmale	74.58 n = 263
Morningness-Eveningness Preference	Morning type	71.58 n = 259
	Intermediate type	70.81 n = 254
	Evening type	68.52 n = 107

The first problem of the present work was to examine whether the subject showing low neuroticism would differ significantly in their academic performance than the subjects showing high neuroticism. Those who score high on neuroticism factor are sensitive, nervous, worrying, insecure, upset, temperamental and gloomy, emotionally unstable and those who score low on neuroticism factor are secure, confident, secure, relaxed, hardy and emotionally stable. Therefore, it was hypothesized that the subjects with low neuroticism would show high academic performance than the subjects with high neuroticism.

Table No. - 5.3

Summary of three way analysis of variance for the data

Source	Sum of Square	Df	Mean Square	F Ratio	Sig
Neuroticism	1764.112	1	1764.112	20.738	.000**
Gender	4971.411	1	4971.411	58.441	.000**
M-E Preference	583.086	2	291.543	3.427	.030*
Neuroticism *Gender	425.454	1	425.454	5.001	.026*
		2	165.992	1.951	.143
Gender* M-E Preference	331.983				
		2	346.724	4.076	.017**
Neuroticism *M-E Preference	693.448	2	129.106	1.518	.220
Neuroticism * Gender *M-E Preference	258.212	608	85.068		
Error	51721.290				
Total	3165529.000	620			

An observation of table-5.2, figure-1 findings indicated that the average academic performance scores of the students of high and low neuroticism are 69.10 and 72.31 respectively, and the obtained F- ratio for the personality factor found to be significant, $F (1, 608) = 20.738, p < .01$ level (table-5.3). The significant F-ratio indicated that the personality factor neuroticism has the significant effect on academic performance of the students. It means the students who had high scores in neuroticism show low academic performance as compared to those with low scores in neuroticism. Thus, the obtained results have confirmed the hypothesis i.e., the subjects with low neuroticism would show high academic performance than the subjects with high neuroticism.

The possible reason of neurotic individuals showing lower academic performance is due to the piece of evidence that the students who have anger, anxiety and are emotionally not strong show not as good academic outcomes. Emotionally unstable are more worried and have propensity to focal point on their "emotional state and self-talk, consequently interfering with attention to academic tasks", thus reducing performance **(De Raad & Schouwenburg, 1996)**. Neurotic personalities have a propensity to show fear, anger, sadness, shyness and emotional inregulations. The present study supported the findings of **Pullmann and Allik (2007)** who had reported the negative correlation between academic performance and neuroticism **(Chamorro-Premuzic & Furnham, 2003; Ciorbea & Pasarica, 2013; Duff, Boyle, Dunleave & Furguson, 2003; Hakimi et al., 2011; Hoque et al., 2010; Laidra, Pullman Allik, 2006; Lathey, 1991; Rogers, 2005; Sanchez-Marin et al., 2001; Trapmann Hell, Hirn and Schuler, 2007).** Neuroticism correlated with academic achievement, particularly for the factor of impulsivity and anxiety **(Kuncel et al., 2005; O'Connor & Paunonen, 2007)**. The personality traits impulsivity has been most consistently related to academic achievement **(Romano, Babchishin, Pagani & Kohen, 2010; Valiente, Eisenberg, Spinrad, Haugen, Thompson & Kupfer, 2013; Vigil-Colct & Morales-Vives, 2005.) Fink and McCown (1993)** reported that the impulsivity seems to be inversely related to academic performance and associated with learning problems consequently, high impulsivity in adolescence show negative relation of academic performance. **Wright (2008)** reported that Emotional stability is positively related to academic performance. Emotional stability positively associated with performance **(Judge & Bono, 2002; Robbins et al., 2004)**. **Furnham, Chamorro-Premuzic and McDougall (2003)** stated that the relation between academic performance and neuroticism is generally implicit in terms of anxiety, mainly under stressful conditions like examination fear and perform better in classroom and examination and show negative relation with academic performance. **Laidra et al., (2007)** also reported that neuroticism negatively associated with GPA in about every grade. Rather, **Farsides and Woodfield (2003)** indicated that neuroticism negatively associated at college students.

Gender (male and female) was considered as the second independent variable. It was assumed that the female would show higher academic performance than male. An observation of table-5.2, figure-2 findings indicated that the average academic performance scores of the male and female students are 67.90 and 74.58 respectively, and the obtained F-ratio for the gender was significant at $F(1, 608) = 58.441$, $p < .01$ level (table-5.3). The significant F-ratio indicates that the gender significantly affect the academic performance of students. The female students show higher academic performance as compared to male students. Thus obtained results have confirmed the hypothesis that the female subjects would show high academic performance than the male subjects. This result confirmed the findings of various other investigators **(Fergusson & Horwood 1997; Praat, 1999; Hillman & Rothman, 2003; Weaver-Hightower, 2003).** Gender difference plays a significant role in all the affairs of human behaviour and so does in respect of their performance. The gender difference in academic performance has been an extensive issue in the area of education. "Gender is the properties that distinguish organism on the basis of their reproductive roles as male or female" **(Abubakar & Uboh, 2010).** In general, boys performance was not good in school and college level as compared to girls. Leonard and **Jiang (1999)** suggest that females have better study skills than the male students. **Spelke (2005); Hyde and Linn (2006)** found that males have not preformed better than females in science and mathematics. The overall performance of the female student show better than the male students **(Mirza & Mallik, 2000; Rana, 2002) and Rana (2002)** also found that the science performance of girls is better than the science performance of the boys. **Amitava, Maojit, Saawata and Braja (2010)** found that the students gender influence their academic performance and they also reveal that the boys perform poorly as compared to girls. Boys are more under achieving students than girls **(McCall, 1994)**. Females show better performance than males **(Escribano, Iaz-Morales, Delgdo & Collado, 2011; Mirza**

& Malik, 2000). McCall (1994) Boys are more under achieving students than girls. The study of **Epstein, Elwood, Hey and Maw De (1998) and Wong, Lam, and Ho (2002)** reveal that boy's performance was not good as compared to girls. **De Baz (1994)** findings suggested a significant gender effect in the favour of male students on academic performance. The female students are outperforming than male students at school, college and university level **(Allon-Lee & Paat, 2001; Mullies, Martin, Gonzalez, & Kennedy, 2003)**. The study of Mishra and Jha (2014) also supported the findings of the present study i.e., female students show better performance as compared to male students.

Morningness-Eveningness Preference i.e., morning type, intermediate type and evening type was considered as the third independent variable. It was assumed that the subjects with morning preference would show higher academic performance than subjects with evening preference and subjects with intermediate preference would remain in between the above two. An observation of table-5.2, figure-3 findings indicated that the average academic performance scores of the morning type, intermediate type and evening type students are 71.58, 70.81 and 68.52 respectively, and the obtained F-ratio for the morningness-eveningness preference were found to be significant at $F (2, 608) = 3.427, p < .05$ level (table-5.3). Significant F-ratio indicated that the morningness-eveningness preference significantly influence the academic performance of the students. The morning types perform better as compared to intermediate type and the intermediate type perform better than the evening type subjects. Thus the obtained results have confirmed the hypothesis that the subjects with morning preference would show higher academic performance than subjects with evening preference and subjects with intermediate preference would remain in between the above two. These results corroborate with the findings from other studies on this topic such as **Franzisp, Anastasiya, Sandra and Richard (2011)** indicated that eveningness negatively related to academic performance and morningness show positive relation with academic performance.

Humans are normally active in the daytime in our culture as compared to afternoon and evening time. Morningness–Eveningness preference that is morning active type or evening active type or intermediate type person has been found to be capable of explaining the variation in the expression of biological and behavioural patterns. In the Indian context, lifestyle of many cultures and families awake in early morning and the tendency or thinking of the one and all, that morning time is the best period for learning and those people who studied in the morning time perform better, and most of the students prefer to go to bed earlier and awoke early in the morning for the studies but in the present circumstances the students tendency is different in this way of learning preference. The morningness-eveningness preference of students affects their academic performance **(Goldstein, Hahn, Hasher, Wiprzycka & Zelazo, 2006; Hines, 2004)**. Most of the findings demonstrated that an adult student shows better performance in the morning than later in the day and evening time show bad performance than the morning and afternoon time **(Hasher, Goldstein & May, 2005; Itons-Peterson, Rocchi, West, McLellan & Hackney, 1998; May, 1999). Besoluk, Onder and Deveci (2011)** found that students with morning preference achieved higher scores than evening preference. **Preckel, Lipnevich, Schneider and Roberts (2011)** indicated that the eveningness was positively related to individuals' cognitive ability and negatively related to academic achievement. Morningness had a negative relationship with cognitive ability and a positive correlation with academic indicators. Morning type students performed better than evening type students **(Besoluk, 2010). Randal and Frech (2009)** findings suggested that student with morning preferences performed better in school achievement. **Robert, Robert and Duong (2009)** findings suggested that the eveningness associated with poor academic performance.

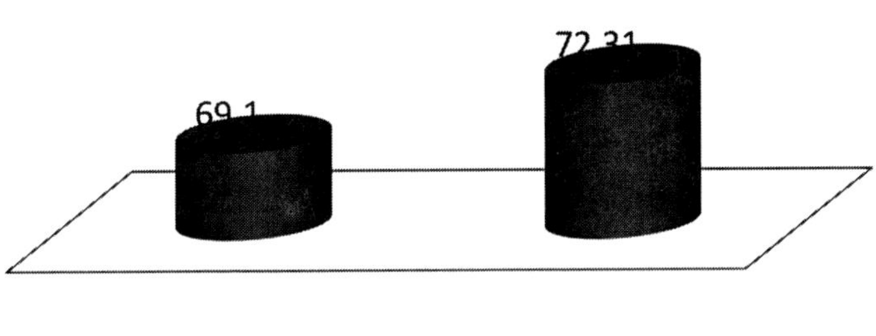

Figure - 1: (Personality) average academic performance scores of high and low neuroticism.

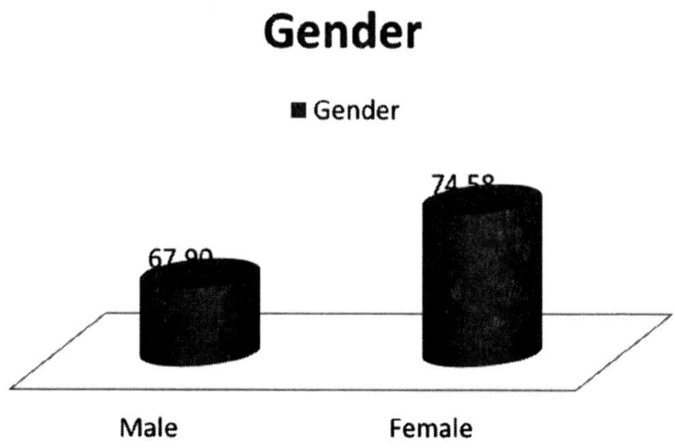

Figure - 2: (Gender) average academic performance scores of male and female

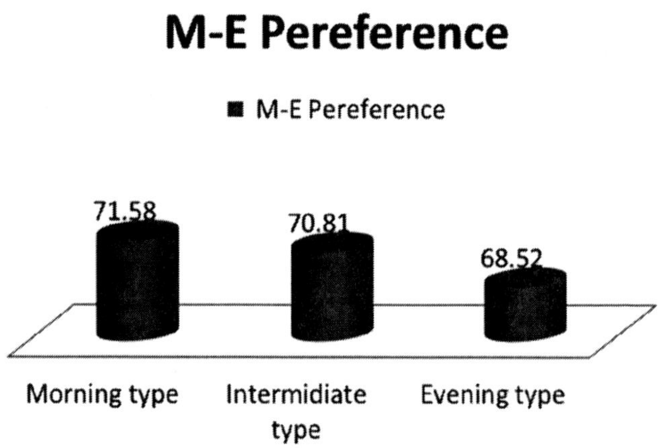

Figure - 3: (Morningness-Eveningness Preference) average academic performance scores of morning type, intermediate type and evening type.

So for, we have discussed the interaction between the independent variables i.e., personality (Neuroticism), gender and morningness-eveningness preference. It would also be useful and important information if the joint effect of any two or more factors is studied. The greatest advantage we get from the analysis of variance technique is that it provides an opportunity to examine the interaction between two or more variables at a time.

Here, in the three-way ANOVA, we get three first-order interactions between any two factors, and second-order interaction among all the three factors.

Table No. -5.4

Average academic performance scores of the subjects of four subgroups formed on the basis of personality (Neuroticism) and gender

Personality (Neuroticism)	Gender	
	Male	Female
High	M = 66.90 SD = 9.848 n = 157	M = 71.45 SD = 9.252 n = 148
Low	M = 68.69 SD = 9.802 n = 200	M = 78.61 SD = 7.441 n = 115

The first order interaction is between personality (Neuroticism) and gender. The average academic performance score of four subgroups formed on the basis of personality (Neuroticism) and gender are shown in table-5.4, figure-4. Result of the ANOVA in table-5.3 findings indicated that the interaction between personality (Neuroticism) and gender were found to be significant $F (1, 608) = 5.001$, $p < .05$ level (table-5.3). This significant interaction suggested that the joint effect of personality (high and low) and gender (male and female) has generated significant variance upon academic performance. The findings of this interaction revealed that the female students were more neurotic as compared to male but their academic performance was better than male students. The result was supported by the findings of Vianello, Schnabel, Sriram and Nosek (2013) who had reported that female students was more neurotic as compared to male students. Shokri, Daneshvarpour and Azam (2008) reported that the personality factor neuroticism show a mediating effect of gender and academic performance. The findings of Lange and Randler (2011) also supported the findings of present study; they reported that girls had more emotional problems then boys.

Table No. -5.5

Average academic performance scores of the subjects of six subgroups formed on the basis of gender and M-E preference

Gender	M-E preference		
	Morning type	Intermediate type	Evening type
Male	M = 68.07 SD = 9.984 n = 145	M = 68.10 SD = 9.513 n = 143	M = 67.14 SD = 10.346 n = 69
Female	M = 76.04 SD = 9.732 n = 114	M = 74.30 SD = 8.637 n = 111	M = 71.03 SD = 8.346 n = 38

The first-order interaction between gender and morningness-eveningness preference was also studied. The average academic performance scores of four subgroups formed on the basis of gender and morningness-eveningness preference are shown in table-5.5. Result of the ANOVA in table-5.3 findings indicated that the interaction between gender and morningness-eveningness preference was not significant F (2, 608) = 1.951 = .143 (table-5.3). This insignificant interaction suggested that the academic performance scores of students of gender i.e., male and female are not dependent upon the morningness-eveningness preference i.e., morning type, intermediate type and evening type. It may be said that the academic performance scores of male and female students do not depend on the level of morningness-eveningness preference.

Table No. -5.6

Average academic performance scores of the subjects of four subgroups formed on the basis of personality (Neuroticism) and M-E preference

Personality (Neuroticism)	M-E preference		
	Morning type	Intermediate type	Evening type
High	M = 68.70 SD = 10.224 n = 122	M = 70.06 SD = 9.140 n = 128	M = 67.76 SD = 10.358 n = 55
Low	M = 74.13 SD = 10.346 n = 137	M = 71.56 SD = 10.082 n = 126	M = 69.33 SD = 9.252 n = 52

The first-order interaction between personality and morningness-eveningness preference was also studied. The average academic performance scores of six subgroups formed on the basis of personality and morningness-eveningness preference are shown in table-5.6, figure-5. Result of the ANOVA in table-5.3 findings indicated that the interaction between personality and morningness-eveningness preference were found to be significant F (2, 608) = 4.076, p > .01 level (table-5.3). This significant interaction suggested that the joint effect of personality (high and low) and morningness-eveningness preference (morning type, intermediate type and evening type) has generated a significant variance upon academic performance. The present results reveal that the low neurotic subjects with morningness preference show better academic performance as compared to other preferences, and highly neurotic shows less performance in every preference. These findings were supported by the work of **Hess, Sherman and Goodman (2000)** who had reported that the neuroticism positively related with eveningness and the findings of **DeYoung, Peterson and Higgins (2002)** reveal that stability positively related with morningness preference. The morningness preference negatively related to impulsivity and trait anxiety **(Caci, Robert & Boyer, 2004)**. This finding shows the relation between neuroticism and morningness-eveningness preference but does not show joint influence on academic performance. The study of **Caci, Adan, Bohle, Natale, Pornpitakpan and Tilley (2005)** reported that the subjects who have higher eveningness preference show more impulsivity.

Table No. -5.7

Average academic performance scores of the subjects of twelve subgroups formed on the basis of personality (Neuroticism), gender and morningnes-eveningness preference

Per-sonal-ity	Gender					
	Male Preference			Female Preference		
(Neu-roti-cism)	Morning Type	Inter-mediate Type	Evening Type	Morn-ing Type	Inter-mediate Type	Evening Type
High	M = 66.18 SD = 10.240 n = 61	M = 68.15 SD = 8.982 n = 66	M = 65.60 SD = 10.839 n = 30	M = 71.23 SD = 9.643 n = 61	M = 72.10 SD = 8.933 n = 62	M = 70.36 SD = 9.304 n = 25
Low	M = 69.44 SD = 9.623 n = 84	M = 68.05 SD = 10.004 n = 77	M = 68.33 SD = 9.927 n = 39	M = 81.57 SD = 6.344 n = 53	M = 77.08 SD = 7.441 n = 49	M = 72.31 SD = 6.237 n = 13

The second-order interaction gives a joint effect of personality, gender and morningness-eveningness preference on academic performance. The average academic performance score of the students of twelve subgroups formed on the basis of personality (high and low), gender (male and female) and morningness-eveningness preference (morning type, intermediate type and evening type) is shown in table-5.7. The obtained F-ratio was not significant $F(2, 608) = 1.518 = .220$ (table-5.3). This insignificant interaction concluded that the difference in academic performance exhibited by the students of low and high personality does not differ significantly because of different level of gender and morningness-eveningness preference.

Thus, the above discussion makes it understandable that all the three factors i.e., personality, gender and morningness-eveningness preference affect the academic performance independently, the interaction between gender and personality and personality and morningness-eveningness preference was found to be significant but no interaction was seen between gender and morningness-eveningness preference. However, the second order interaction is not found to be significant.

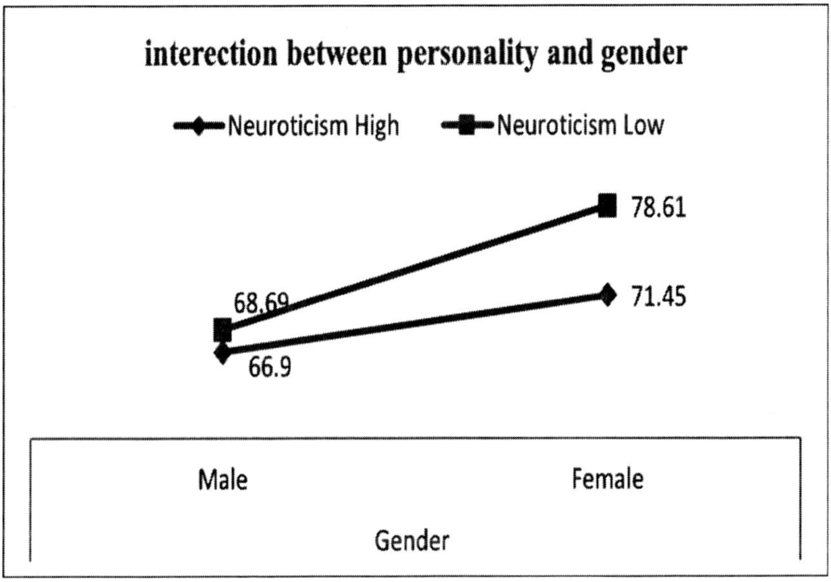

Figure - 4: Average academic performance scores of four subgroups formed on the basis of personality and gender

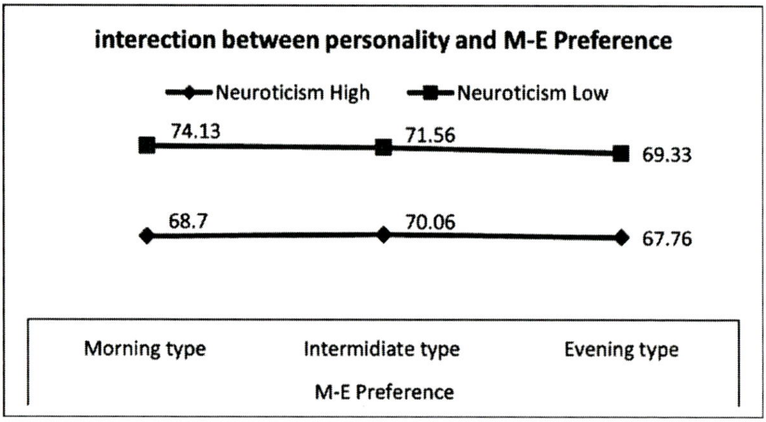

Figure – 5: Average academic performance scores of four subgroups formed on the basis of personality and morningness-eveningness preference

Personality Factor Extraversion

Table No. -5.8

Average academic performance scores of the groups of personality (Extraversion), gender and morningnes-eveningness preference

Variables	Groups	Average Scores of Academic Performance
Personality (Extraversion)	High	72.77 n = 365
	Low	70.91 n = 302
Gender	Male	70.43 n = 373
	Female	73.83 n = 294
Morningness-Eveningness Preference	Morning type	72.64 n = 272
	Intermediate type	71.65 n = 279
	Evening type	70.93 n = 116

The second problem of the present work was to examine whether the subject showing low extraversion differ significantly in their academic performance than the subjects showing high extraversion. Those who score high on extraversion factor are talkative, adventurous, frank, assertive, outgoing, energetic, fun loving and sociable and those who score low on extraversion factor are introvert, withdrawn, quiet, shy, reserved and unsociable. Therefore, it was hypothesized that the subjects with low extraversion would show low academic performance than the subjects with high extraversion.

Table No. -5.9

Summary of three way analysis of variance for the data

Source	Sum of Square	df	Mean Square	F Ratio	Sig
Extraversion	437.051	1	437.051	5.009	.026*
Gender	1147.348	1	1147.348	13.151	.000**
M-E Preference	161.525	2	80.762	.926	.397
Extraversion * Gender	14.841	1	14.841	.170	.680
Gender* M-E Preference	147.954	2	73.977	.848	.429
Extraversion * M-E Preference	266.259	2	133.130	1.526	.218
Extraversion *Gender *M-E Preference	159.980	2	79.990	.917	.400
Error	57145.277	655	87.245		
Total	**3511370.000**	**667**			

An observation of table-5.8, figure-6 findings indicated that the average academic performance scores of the students of high and low extraversion are 72.77 and 70.91 respectively, and the obtained F-ratio for the personality factor were found to be significant, F (1, 655) = 5.009, $p < .05$ level (table-5.9). The significant F-ratio indicates that the personality factor extraversion has a significant effect on academic performance of the students. It means the students who have high scores in extraversion show high academic performance as compared to those who have low scores in extraversion. Thus, the obtained results have confirmed the hypothesis. The possible explanation of the extrovert students showing better performance is due to the information that the extrovert students keep themselves friendly, optimistic, sociable, experience positive emotions and high activity. Extravert students interact more in the class with their teachers and peers. They enjoy participating in gathering, group discussions and engineering education involves a large number of activities i.e., group discussions, seminars, team-based projects, etc. The results of the present research work are in the support of extraverts. Such kinds of interactions with others, helped these students, in getting more ideas from others, as well as getting their problems, related to academics, easily sorted out and extravert students outperformed in academic tasks **(Furnham & Medhurst, 1995; De Fruyt & Mervielde, 1996)** also suggested a positive association between extraversion and academic performance. The present research work supported the previous findings that extraversion is a successful positive predictor of academic performance **(Lievens, Cortsier, Defruyt & De Maessneer, 2002; Schniederjan et al., 2005)**. Extravert performed better in oral examination **(Chamorro-Premuzic & Furnham, 2003; Furnham & Medhurst, 1995; Robinson, Gabriel, & Katchan, 1993)**. A little amount of the studies suggested that the personality trait extraversion is positively related with academic performance **(Busto et al, 1999; Chowdhury, 2006; Eysenck 1992; Felder& Felder & Dietz, 2002; Furnham et al., 2009; Furnham, Forde & Cotter, 1998; FuSalehi, Khak & Alam, 2013; Rosthstin et al., 1994; Shokri, Kadivar, Naghsh, Daneshvarpour & Molaei, 2007). De Raad and Schouwenburg (1996)** stated that those students who are high extravert will perform better academically. **De Raad and Schouwenburg (1996)** suggested that those students who are extravert perform better academically because of higher energy levels, along with a positive attitude leading to a desire to learn and understand.

Gender (male and female) was considered as the second independent variable. It was assumed that the female would show higher academic performance than male. An observation of table-5.8, figure-7 findings indicated that the average academic performance scores of male and female students are 69.10 and 74.58 respectively, and the obtained result of the gender were found to be significant at F (2, 655) = 13.151, p < .01 level (table-5.9). The significant F-ratio indicated that the gender significantly affected the academic performance of students. The female students show higher academic performance as compared to male students. In this way, obtained results have confirmed the hypothesis that the female subjects would show high academic performance than the male subjects. In the previous part of the present study we have already seen that the gender affects the academic performance i.e., **(Abubakar & Uboh, 2010; Allon-Lee & Paat, 2001; Amitava, Maojit, Saawata and Braja, 2010; Delgdo & Collado, 2011; Epstein, Elwood, Hey and Maw De, 1998; Escribano, Iaz-Morales, Fergusson & Horwood 1997; Hyde and Linn, 2006; Mirza & Malik, 2000; Mishra & Jha, 2014; Mullies, Martin, Gonzalez, & Kennedy, 2003; Rana, 2002; Spelke, 2005; Weaver-Hightower, 2003; Wong, Lam, and Ho, 2002)** who observed that the female students perform better as compared to male students. However, the findings of the present study reveal that the female show higher academic performance than male.

Morningness-Eveningness Preference i.e., morning type, intermediate type and evening type was considered as the third independent variable. It was assumed that the subjects with morning preference would show higher academic performance than the subjects with evening preference and subjects with intermediate preference would remain in between the above two. An observation of table-5.8, figure-8 findings indicated that the average academic performance scores of morning type, intermediate type and evening type students are 72.64, 71.65 and 70.93 respectively, and the obtained F-ratio for the morningness-eveningness preference was not significant at F (2, 655) = .926 = .397 (table-5.9). This insignificant F-ratio indicated that the academic performance of the students was not affected by the morningness-eveningness preference. Thus, the obtained results have not confirmed the hypothesis.

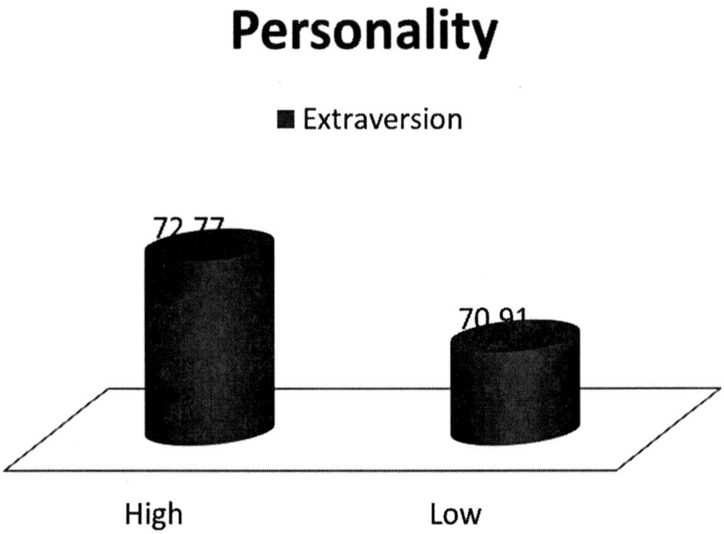

Figure – 6: (Personality) average academic performance scores of high and low Extraversion.

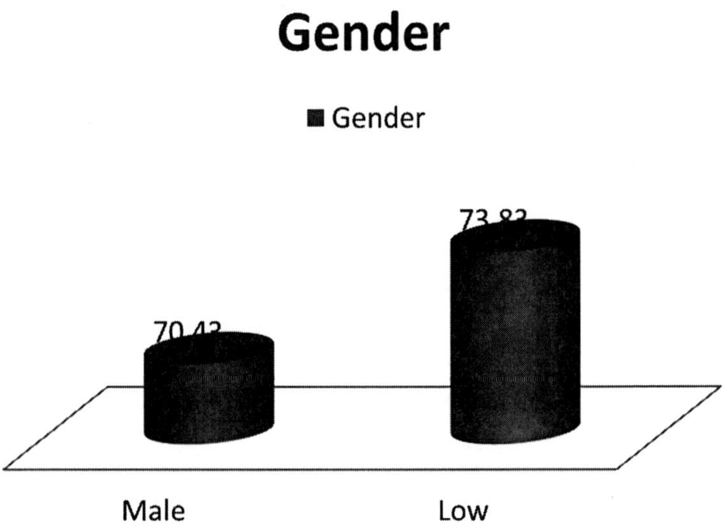

Figure – 7: (Gender) average academic performance scores of male and female.

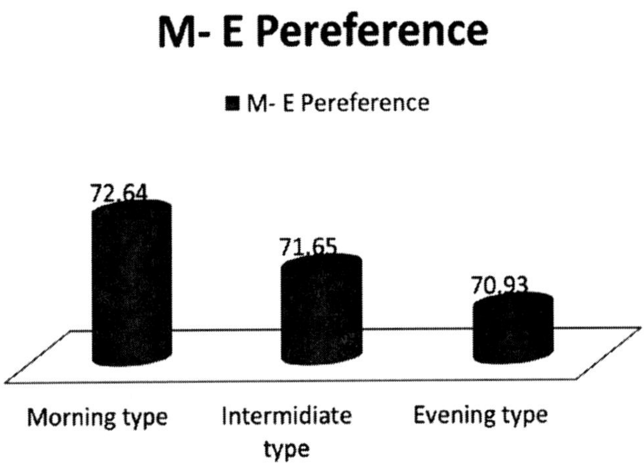

Figure – 8: (M-E Preference) average academic performance scores of morning type, intermediate type and evening type.

So for, we have discussed the interaction between the independent variables i.e. personality (extraversion), gender and morningness-eveningness preference.

Table No. -5.10

Average academic performance scores of the subjects of four subgroups formed on the basis of personality (Extraversion) and gender

Personality (Neuroticism)	Gender	
	Male	Female
High	M = 70.99 SD = 9.050 n = 212	M = 75.24 SD = 9.179 n = 153
Low	M = 69.69 SD = 10.390 n = 161	M = 72.31 SD = 8.660 n = 141

The first order interaction is between personality (extraversion) and gender. The average academic performance score of four subgroups formed on the basis of personality (extraversion) and gender are shown in table-5.10. Result of the ANOVA in table-5.9 findings indicated that the interaction between personality (extraversion) and gender was not significant F (1, 655) = .170 = .680 (table-5.9). This insignificant interaction suggested that the academic performance of the students' high and low extravert do not depend on gender. It may be said that the insignificant F-ratio prove that both factors - personality and gender –are independent in exerting their influence on academic performance.

Table No. -5.11

Average academic performance scores of the subjects of four subgroups formed on the basis of gender and M-E preference

Gender	M-E preference		
	Morning type	Intermediate type	Evening type
Male	M = 70.62 SD = 10.423 n = 106	M = 71.44 SD = 8.886 n = 134	M = 70.27 SD = 10.171 n = 62
Female	M = 73.93 SD = 9.578 n = 166	M = 71.83 SD = 9.409 n = 145	M = 71.69 SD = 8.002 n = 54

The first-order interaction between gender and morningness-eveningness preference was also studied. The average academic performance scores of four subgroups formed on the basis of gender and morningness-eveningness preference are shown in table-5.11. Result of the ANOVA in table-5.9 findings indicated that the interaction between gender and morningness-eveningness preference was not significant F (2, 655) =

.848 = .429 (table-5.9). This insignificant interaction suggested that the academic performance scores of students of gender i.e., male and female are not dependent upon the morningness-eveningness preference i.e., morning type, intermediate type and evening type. It may be said that the academic performance scores of male and female students do not depend on the level of morningness-eveningness preference.

Table No. -5.12

Average academic performance scores of the subjects of four subgroups formed on the basis of personality (Extraversion) and M-E preference

Personality (Neuroticism)	M-E preference		
	Morning type	Intermediate type	Evening type
High	M = 72.12 SD = 9.914 n = 153	M = 69.68 SD = 9.241 n = 149	M = 70.38 SD = 9.970 n = 71
Low	M = 74.53 SD = 9.893 n = 119	M = 73.90 SD = 8.529 n = 130	M = 71.80 SD = 7.902 n = 45

The first-order interaction between personality and morningness-eveningness preference was also studied. The average academic performance scores of four subgroups formed on the basis of personality and morningness-eveningness preference are shown in table-5.12. Result of the ANOVA in table-5.9 findings indicated that the interaction between personality and morningness-eveningness preference was not significant F (2, 655) = 1.526 = .218 (table-5.9). This insignificant interaction suggested that the academic performance scores of students of the high and low extravert do not depend on morningness-eveningness preference.

Table No. -5.13

Average academic performance scores of the subjects of twelve subgroups formed on the basis of personality (Extraversion), gender and morningnes-eveningness preference

Personality (Extraversion)	Gender					
	Male Preference			Female Preference		
(Neuroticism)	Morning Type	Intermediate Type	Evening Type	Morning Type	Intermediate Type	Evening Type
High	M = 72.12 SD = 9.186 n = 94	M = 69.36 SD = 9.456 n = 81	M = 70.68 SD = 7.318 n = 37	M = 76.31 SD = 9.622 n = 72	M = 74.71 SD = 8.423 n = 64	M = 71.71 SD = 9.571 n = 17
Low	M = 69.68 SD = 10.889 n = 59	M = 70.06 SD = 9.034 n = 68	M = 68.97 SD = 12.187 n = 34	M = 71.81 SD = 9.793 n = 47	M = 72.86 SD = 8.566 n = 66	M = 71.86 SD = 6.889 n = 28

The second-order interaction gives a joint effect of personality, gender and morningness-eveningness preference. The average academic performance scores of the students of twelve subgroups were formed on the basis of personality (high and low), gender (male and female) and morningness-eveningness preference (morning type, intermediate type and evening type) shown in the table-5.13. The obtained F-ratio was not significant F (2, 655) = .917 = .400 (table-9). This insignificant interaction concluded that the difference in academic performance exhibited by the students of low and high personality does not differ significantly because of different level of gender and morningness-eveningness preference.

Therefore, the above discussion makes it understandable that all the three factors i.e., personality and gender affect the academic performance independently and the academic performance of the students are not affected by the morningness-eveningness preference. However, none of their interaction is found to be significant at any level.

Personality Factor Openness

Table No. -5.14

Average academic performance scores of the groups of personality (Openness), gender and morningnes-eveningness preference

Variables	Groups	Average Scores of Academic Performance
Personality (Openness)	High	72.60 n = 334
	Low	71.07 n = 318
Gender	Male	68.67 n = 361
	Female	5.79 n = 291
Morningness-Eveningness Preference	Morning type	73.01 n = 279
	Intermediate type	71.61 n = 266
	Evening type	69.45 n = 107

The third problem is to examine whether the subjects showing low openness differ significantly in their academic performance than the subjects showing high openness. Those who score high on openness have broad interests and are inventive, curious and complex and those who score low on openness factor are traditional, cautious, narrow interest, old-fashioned and prefer familiarity, and are uncreative and down to earth. Therefore, it was hypothesized that the subjects with low openness would show low academic performance than the subjects with high openness.

Table No. -5.15

Summary of three way analysis of variance for the data

Source	Sum of Square	df	Mean Square	F Ratio	Sig
Openness	393.001	1	393.001	4.935	.027*
Gender	5867.034	1	5867.034	73.665	.000**
M-E Preference	853.622	2	4.26.811	5.359	.005**
Openness * Gender	35.455	1	35.455	.445	.505
Gender* M-E Preference	489.859	2	244.930	3.075	.047*
Openness * M-E Preference	90.311	2	45.156	.567	.568*
Openness *Gender * M-E*Preference	289.124	2	144.562	1.815	.164
Error	50972.374	640	79.644		
Total	**61412.569**	**652**			

An observation of table-5.14, figure-9 findings indicated that the average academic performance scores of the students of high and low openness are 72.60 and 71.07 respectively, and the obtained F-ratio for the personality factor was found to be significant, $F(1, 640) = 4.935$, $p < .05$ level (table-5.15). The significant F-ratio indicated that the personality factor openness has a significant effect on academic performance of the students. It means the students who have high scores in openness show high academic performance as compared to those who have low scores in openness. Thus the obtained results have confirmed the hypothesis that students who have high openness perform better in academics. The present research work supported the previous findings of the (**Chowdhury, 2006; Farsides & Woodfield, 2003; Geisler-Brenstein & Schmeck, 1996; Gow, 2004; Gray & Watson, 2002; Komarraju, Karau & Schmeck, 2009; Lievens et al., 2002; McKenzie & Phillips et al., 2003; Melissa, O'Connor & Sampo, 2007; Rogers, 2005; Rothstein, Paunonen, Rush & King, 1994; Wright, 2008)** who had reported that openness to be positively related to academic performance. The role of openness is an important personality factor that predicts academic performance **(Busato, Prins, Elshout & Hamaker 1999; Komarraju & Karau, 2005; Komarraju, Karau, & Schmeck, 2009; Shokri, Danedhvarpour, Askari, 2008; Laidra et. al., 2007; Viari, Rad &Torabi, 2011)** because the students who have high scores in openness have a strong intellectual curiosity, are more imaginative, creative, inventive and interested **(Komarraju, Karau, Schmeck & Avdic, 2011)** thus they always think of new ideas and creativity and curiosity and is also a good predictor for academic performance. Openness is also related to better scores in vocabulary and general knowledge **(Ackerman & Heggestad, 1997; Ashton, Lee, Vernon, & Jang, 2000; Goff & Ackerman, 1992)**. Openness is positively linked with learning approaches **(Vermetten, Lodewijks & Vermunt, 2001)**, learning motivation **(Tempelaar, Gijselaers, van der Loeff, & Nijhuis, 2007)** and critical thinking **(Bidjerano & Dai, 2007) Farsides and Woodfield (2003)** indicated that openness has been positively associated with grades. **Vikanda, et al., (2012)** reported that openness predict positive relation with cognitive and affective academic performance.

Gender (male and female) was considered as the second independent variable. It was assumed that female would show higher academic performance than male. An observation of table-5.14, figure-10 findings indicated that the average academic performance scores of the male and female students are 68.67 and 75.79 respectively, and the obtained F-ratio for the gender found to be significant at $F(1, 640) = 73.665$, $p < .01$ level (table-5.15). The significant F-ratio indicated that gender significantly affects the academic performance of students. The female students show higher academic performance as compared to male students. In this way obtained results have confirmed the hypothesis that the female subjects would show high academic performance than the male subjects. Result has already been mentioned earlier investigating that the female students show higher academic performance as compared to male students **(Abubakar & Uboh, 2010; Allon-Lee & Paat, 2001; Amitava, Maojit, Saawata and Braja, 2010; Delgdo & Collado, 2011; Epstein, Elwood, Hey and Maw De, 1998; Escribano, Iaz-Morales, Fergusson & Horwood 1997; Hyde and Linn, 2006; Mirza & Malik, 2000; Mishra & Jha, 2014; Mullies, Martin, Gonzalez, & Kennedy, 2003; Rana, 2002; Spelke, 2005; Weaver-Hightower, 2003; Wong, Lam, and Ho, 2002).**

Morningness-Eveningness Preference i.e., morning type, intermediate type and evening type was considered as the third independent variable. It was assumed that the subjects with morning preference would show higher academic performance than subjects with evening preference and subjects with intermediate preference would remain in between the above two. An observation of table-5.14, figure-11 findings indicated that the average academic performance scores of the morning type, intermediate type and evening type student are 73.01, 71.61 and 69.45 respectively, and the obtained F-ratio for the morningness-eveningness preference were found to be significant at $F(2, 640) = 5.359$, $p < .05$ level (table-5.15). A significant F-ratio indicated that the morningness-eveningness preference significantly influenced the academic performance of the students. The morning types perform better as compared to intermediate type and the intermediate type perform better than the evening type subjects. Thus, the obtained results have confirmed the hypothesis. We have already mentioned in our previous studies that the morning active students show higher academic performance as compared to intermediate and evening active students. The study of **(Besoluk, 2010; Besoluk, Onder & Deveci, 2011; Goldstein, Hahn, Hasher, Hines, 2004; Hasher, Goldstein & May, 2005; Itons-Peterson, Rocchi, West, McLellan & Hackney, 1998; May, 1999; Preckel, Lipnevich, Schneider and Roberts, 2011; Randal and Frech, 2009; Wiprzycka & Zelazo, 2006)** supported the findings of the present study i.e., morning active students perform better as compared to intermediate and evening active students. Robert, Robert and Duong (2009) findings suggested that the eveningness associated with poor academic performance.

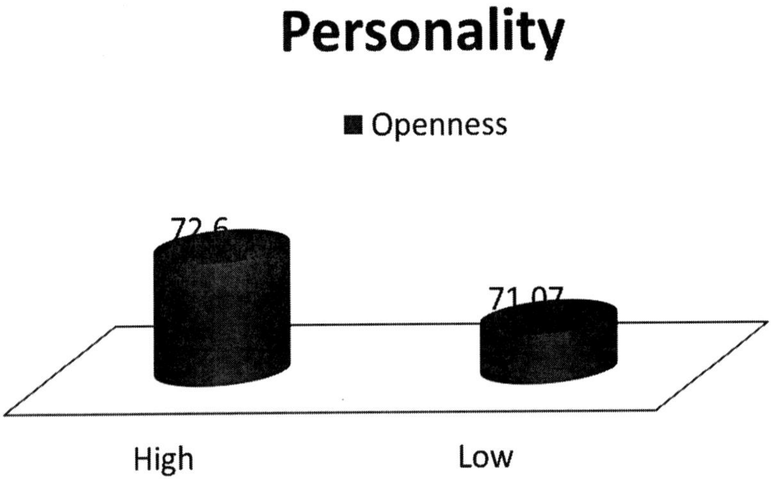

Figure – 9: (Personality) average academic performance scores of high and low Openness

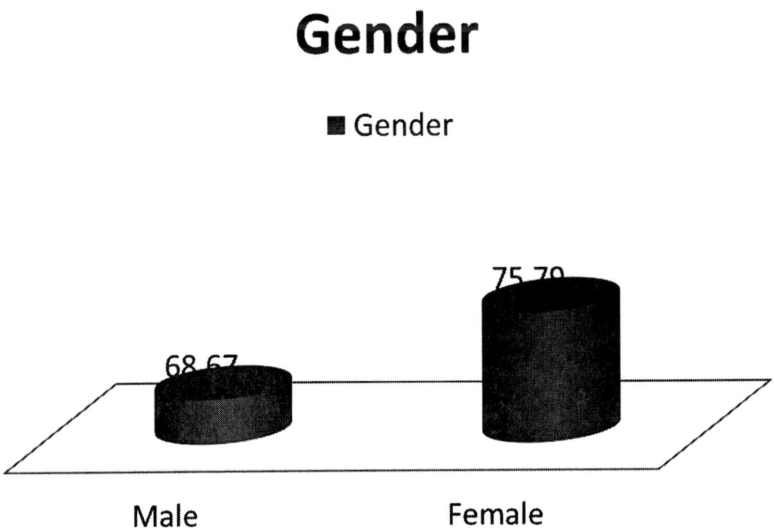

Figure – 10: (Gender) average academic performance scores of male and female

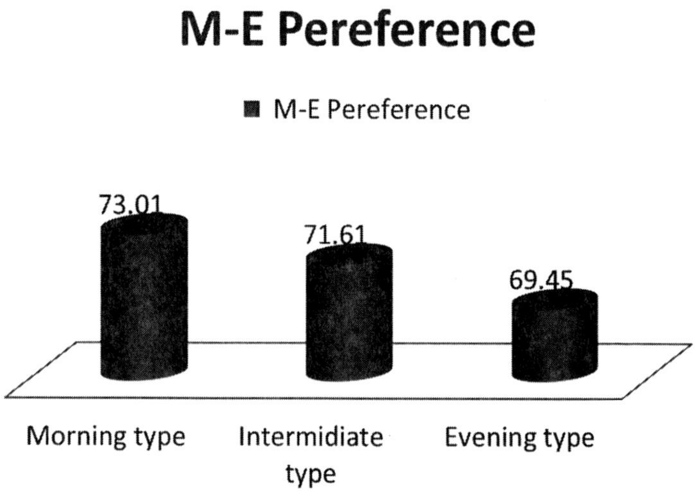

Figure - 11: (Morningness-Evenigness preference) average academic performance scores of morning active, intermediate active and female

So far, we have discussed the interaction between the independent variables i.e., personality (openness), gender and morningness-eveningness preference.

Table No. -5.16

Average academic performance scores of the subjects of four subgroups formed on the basis of personality (Openness) and gender

Personality	Gender	
(Openness)	**Male**	**Female**
High	M = 69.40 SD - 9.176 n = 192	M = 76.92 SD = 8.249 n = 142
Low	M = 67.85 SD = 10.122 n = 169	M = 74.72 SD = 8.132 n = 149

The first order interaction is between personality (Openness) and gender. The average academic performance score of four subgroups formed on the basis of personality (Openness) and gender are shown in table-5.16. Result of the ANOVA in table-5.15 findings indicated that the interaction between personality (Openness) and gender were not found to be significant F (1, 640) = .445 = .505 (table-5.15). This insignificant interaction suggested that the academic performance of the students' high and low openness do not depend on gender. It may be said that the insignificant F-ratio prove that both factors personality and gender are independent in exerting their influence on academic performance.

Table No. -5.17

Average academic performance scores of the subjects of four subgroups formed on the basis of gender and M-E preference

Gender	M-E preference		
	Morning type	**Intermediate type**	**Evening type**
Male	M = 68.89 SD = 9.864 n = 155	M = 69.17 SD = 9.330 n = 140	M = 67.11 SD = 9.784 n = 66
Female	M = 78.15 SD = 8.323 n = 124	M = 74.31 SD = 7.972 n = 126	M = 73.22 SD = 7.122 n = 41

The first-order interaction between gender and morningness-eveningness preference was also studied. The average academic performance scores of four subgroups formed on the basis of gender and morningness-eveningness preference are shown in table-5.17, figure-12. Result of the ANOVA in table-5.15 findings indicated that the interaction between gender and morningness-eveningness preference were found to be significant F (2, 640) = 3.075, $p < .05$ level (table-5.15). This significant interaction suggested that the academic performance scores of students of gender i.e., male and female are dependent upon the morningness-eveningness preference i.e., morning type, intermediate type and evening type. It may be said that the joint effect of gender (male and female) and morningness-eveningness preference (morning type, intermediate type and evening type) has generated a significant variance upon academic performance. The findings of the present research work reveal that female students show better performance as compared to male students in every preference but morning oriented female show better performance as compared to other preferences. Girls mostly show a strong tendency to morningness preference as compared to boys. The present study supported by the findings of **Natale and Danesi (2002)** have reported that boys were more evening active then the girls. Some contradictory findings suggested that boys had shown more morningness preference than the girls **(Diaz-Morales & Sorroche, 2008; Prieto, Diaz-Morales & Barreno, 2012).**

Table No. -5.18

Average academic performance scores of the subjects of four subgroups formed on the basis of personality (Openness) and M-E preference

Personality (Openness)	M-E preference		
	Morning type	Intermediate type	Evening type
High	M = 73.34 SD = 9.948 n = 163	M = 72.23 SD = 9.347 n = 122	M = 71.04 SD = 8.505 n =49
Low	M = 72.54 SD = 10.770 n = 116	M = 71.08 SD = 8.825 n = 144	M = 68.10 SD = 9.81 n = 58

The first-order interaction between personality and morningness-eveningness preference was also studied. The average academic performance scores of four subgroups formed on the basis of personality and morningness-eveningness preference are show in table-5.18. Result of the ANOVA in table-5.15 findings indicated that interaction between personality and morningness-eveningness preference was not significant F (2, 640) = .567, p = .568 (table-5.15). This insignificant interaction suggested that the joint effect of personality (high and low) and morningness-eveningness preference (morning type, intermediate type and evening type) has not generated a significant variance upon academic performance.

Table No. -5.19

Average academic performance scores of the subjects of twelve subgroups formed on the basis of personality (Openness), gender and morningnes-eveningness preference

Per-sonal-ity (Open-ness)	Gender					
	Male Preference			Female Preference		
(Neu-roti-cism)	Morning Type	Inter-mediate Type	Evening Type	Morn-ing Type	Inter-medi-ate Type	Evening Type
High	M = 68.89 SD = 9.864 n = 89	M = 69.17 SD = 9.330 n = 70	M = 67.11 SD = 9.784 n = 66	M = 78.99 SD = 7.842 n = 74	M = 75.06 SD = 8.574 n = 52	M = 73.44 SD = 6.663 n = 16
Low	M = 68.21 SD = 10.920 n = 66	M = 68.21 SD = 9.226 n = 70	M = 64.33 SD = 9.755 n = 33	M = 76.92 SD = 8.926 n = 50	M = 73.78 SD = 7.537 n = 74	M = 73.08 SD = 7.533 n = 25

The second-order interaction gives a joint effect of personality, gender and morningness-eveningness preference. The average academic performance scores of the students of twelve subgroups formed on the basis of personality (high and low), gender (male and female) and morningness-eveningness preference (morning type, intermediate type and evening type) ar shown in the table-5.19. The obtained F-ratio was not significant F (2, 240) = 1.015 = .164 (table-5.15). This insignificant interaction concluded that the difference in academic performance exhibited by the students of low and high personality does not differ significantly because of different level of gender and morningness-eveningness preference.

Thus, the above discussion makes it understandable that all the three factors i.e., personality, gender and morningness-eveningness preference affect the academic performance independently, the interaction between gender and morningness-eveningness preference was found to be significant but no interaction between the gender and personality and between morningness-eveningness preference and personality. However the second-order interaction is found to be not significant.

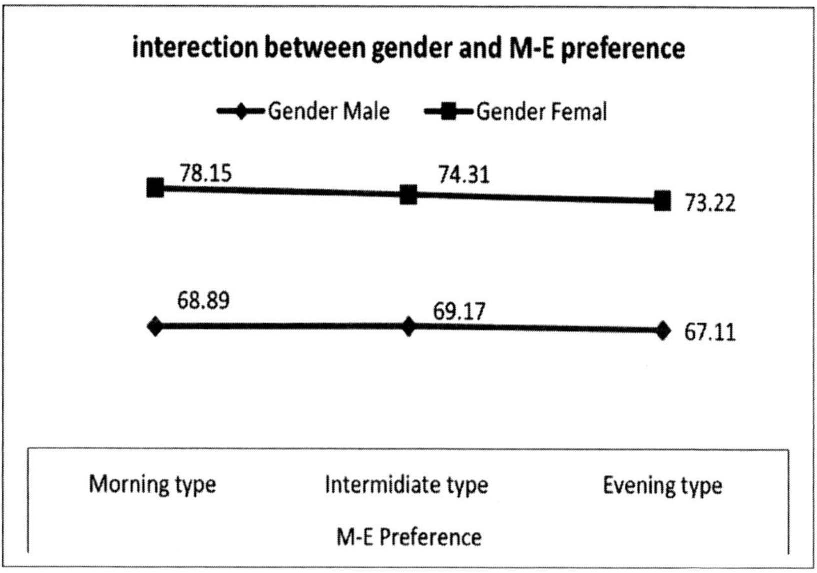

Figure- 12: Average academic performance scores of four subgroups formed on the basis of gender and morningness-eveningness preference

Personality Factor Agreeableness

Table No. -5.20

Average academic performance scores of the groups of personality (Agreeableness), gender and morningnes-eveningness preference

Variables	Groups	Average Scores of Academic Performance
Personality (Agreeableness)	High	70.18 n = 346
	Low	71.09 n = 337
Gender	Male	68.72 n = 395
	Female	73.25 n = 288
Morningness-Eveningness Preference	Morning type	70.12 n = 281
	Intermediate type	71.19 n = 296
	Evening type	70.42 n = 106

The fourth problem of the present work was to examine whether the subjects who show low agreeableness differ significantly in their academic performance than the subjects showing high agreeableness. Those who score high on agreeableness factor are friendly, compassionate, forgiving, courteous altruistic, kind, gentle and sympathetic and those who score low on agreeableness factor are competitive, unfriendly, hostile, indifferent, self-centered, unkind, jealous, critical, harsh, callous and rude. Therefore, it was hypothesized that the subjects with low agreeableness would show low academic performance than the subjects with high agreeableness.

Table No. 5.21

Summary of three way analysis of variance for the data

Source	Sum of Square	df	Mean Square	F Ratio	Sig
Agreeableness	78.600	1	78.600	.950	.330
Gender	1648.914	1	1648.914	19.922	.000**
M-E Preference	51.410	2	25.705	.331	.733
Agreeableness * Gender	1.745	1	1.745	.021	.885
Gender* M-E Preference	503.109	2	251.555	3.039	.049*
Agreeableness * M-E Preference	182.207	2	91.103	1.101	.333
Agreeableness *Gender* M-E Preference	58.761	2	29.380	.355	.701
Error	55536.837	671	82.767		
Total	**3467262.000**	**683**			

An observation of table-5.20, figure-13 findings indicated that the average academic performance scores of the students of high and low agreeableness are 70.18 and 71.09 respectively, and the obtained F-ratio for the personality factor was not significant, F (1, 671) = .950 = .330 (table-5.21). The insignificant F-ratio indicated that the personality factor agreeableness has showed no significant effect on academic performance of the students. It means that the academic performance of the students was not affected by the personality factor agreeableness. Thus, the obtained results have not confirmed the hypothesis. Agreeableness explains the characteristics of sympathetic, trusting and cooperative. Those students' who have high scores on agreeableness are selfless, flexible and pleasant. Those scoring low on this trait find it complicated to get along with others. The findings of the present work supported by the earlier findings of **(Chamorro-Premuzic & Furnham, 2002; & Furnham, Chamorro-Premuzic & McDougall, 2003; Mitrofan & Ion, 2013; Salehi, Khak & Alam, 2013; Troncon, Drammis, Lebella, 2014; Zeidner & Matthews, 2000)** have reported that the agreeableness show no significant linked with academic performance.

Gender (male and female) was considered as the second independent variable. It was assumed that female would show higher academic performance than male. An observation of table-5.20, figure-14 findings indicated that the average academic performance scores of the male and female students are 68.72 and 73.25 respectively, and the obtained F-ratio for the gender found to be significant at , $F(1, 671) = 19.922$, $p < .01$ level (table-5.21). The significant F-ratio indicated that the gender significantly affects the academic performance. The female students show higher academic performance as compared to male students. In this way, the obtained results have confirmed the hypothesis that the female subjects would show high academic performance than the male subjects. We have already discussed in the earlier part of our studies that the gender influences the academic performance **(Abubakar & Uboh, 2010; Allon-Lee & Paat, 2001; Amitava, Maojit, Saawata and Braja, 2010; Delgdo & Collado, 2011; Epstein, Elwood, Hey and Maw De, 1998; Escribano, Iaz-Morales, Fergusson & Horwood 1997; Hyde and Linn, 2006; Mirza & Malik, 2000; Mishra & Jha, 2014; Mullies, Martin, Gonzalez, & Kennedy, 2003; Rana, 2002; Spelke, 2005; Weaver-Hightower, 2003; Wong, Lam, and Ho, 2002)** who have reported that female students show higher academic performance as compared to male students.

Morningness-Eveningness Preference i.e., morning type, intermediate type and evening type was considered as the third independent variable. It was assumed that the subjects with morning preference would show a higher academic performance than the subjects with evening preference and subjects with intermediate preference would remain in between the above two. An observation of table-5.20, figure-15 findings indicated that the average academic performance scores of the morning type, intermediate type and evening type students are 70.12, 71.19 and 70.42 respectively, and the obtained F-ratio for the morningness-eveningness preference was not significant F (2,

671) = .311 = .733 (table-5.21). The insignificant F ratio indicated that the academic performance of the students was not influenced by the morningness-eveningness preference. Thus, the obtained results have not confirmed the hypothesis. The result of the present study support the findings of Diaz-Morales & Sorroche, (2008); Prieto, Diaz-Morales & Barreno (2012) who had suggested that the boys showed more morningness preference than the girls.

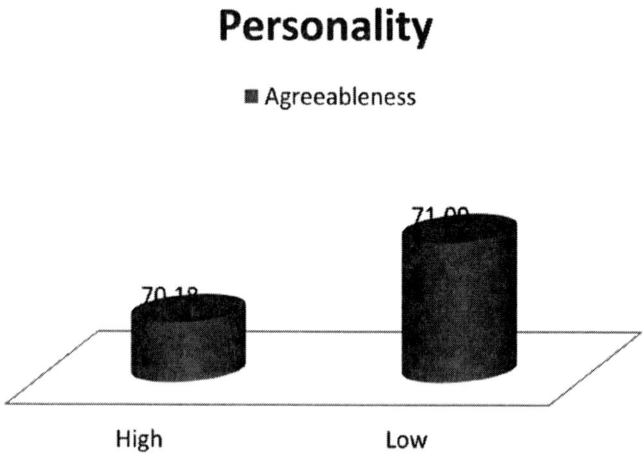

Figure- 13: (Personality) average academic performance scores of high and low agreeableness

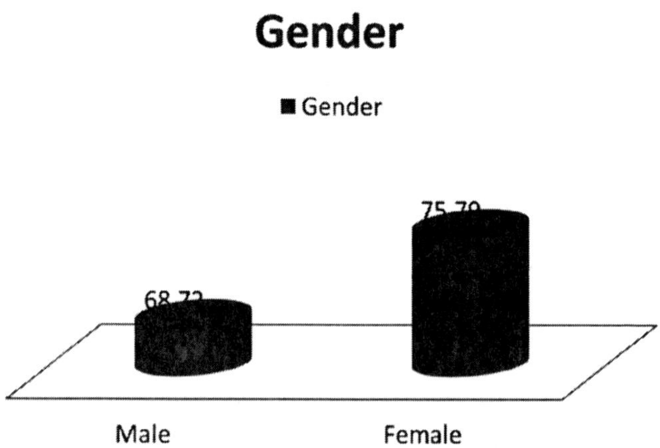

Figure- 14: (Gender) average academic performance scores Of male and female

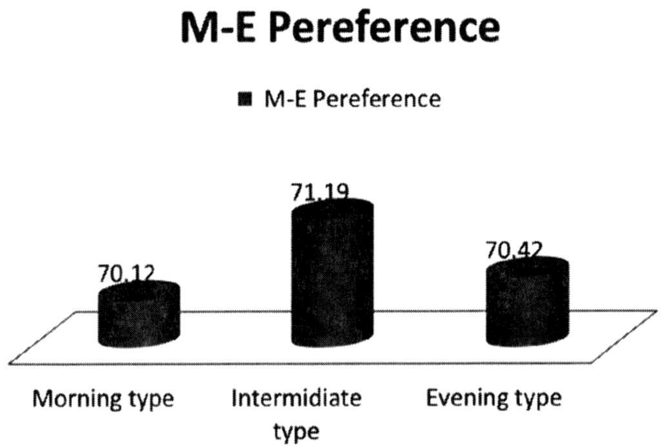

Figure - 15: (Morningness-Evenigness preference) average academic performance scores of morning active, intermediate active and evening active

So far, we have discussed the interaction between the independent variables i.e. personality (agreeableness), gender and morningness-eveningness preference.

Table No. -5.22

Average academic performance scores of the subjects of four subgroups formed on the basis of personality (Agreeableness) and gender

Personality (Agreeableness)	Gender	
	Male	Female
High	M = 67.88 SD = 10.077 n = 186	M = 72.85 SD = 8.999 n = 160
Low	M = 69.47 SD = 8.849 n = 209	M = 73.75 SD = 8.141 n = 128

The first order interaction is between personality (Agreeableness) and gender. The average academic performance score of four subgroups formed on the basis of personality (Agreeableness) and gender are shown in table-5.22. Result of the ANOVA in table-5.21 findings indicated that the interaction between personality (agreeableness) and gender was not significant F (1, 671) = .021 = .885 (table-5.21). This insignificant interaction suggested that the academic performance of the students' high and low agreeableness do not depend on gender. It may be said that the insignificant F-ratio prove that both factors - personality and gender – are independent in exerting their influence on academic performance.

Table No. -5.23

Average academic performance scores of the subjects of four subgroups formed on the basis of gender and M-E preference

Gender	M-E preference		
	Morning type	**Intermediate type**	**Evening type**
Male	M = 68.14 SD = 10.090 n = 164	M = 68.60 SD = 9.078 n = 159	M = 70.29 SD = 8.776 n = 72
Female	M = 72.90 SD = 8.985 n = 117	M = 74.18 SD = 8.212 n = 137	M = 70.71 SD = 8.636 n = 34

The first-order interaction between gender and morningness-eveningness preference was also studied. The average academic performance scores of four subgroups formed on the basis of gender and morningness-eveningness preference are shown in table-5.23, figure-16. Result of the ANOVA in table-5.21 findings indicated that the interaction between gender and morningness-eveningness preference was not significant

F (2, 671) = 3.039, p < .05 level (table-5.21). This significant interaction suggested that the academic performance scores of students of gender i.e., male and female are affected by the morningness-eveningness preference i.e., morning type, intermediate type and evening type. It may be said that the academic performance scores of male and female students depend on the level of morningness-eveningness preference. The findings of the present research work reveal that female students show better performance as compared to male students in every preferences but morning oriented female show better performance as compared to other preferences. Girls mostly show moringness preference as compared to boys. The findings of **Natale and Danesi (2002)** suggested that the boys were more evening active as compared to girls. Some contradictory findings of **Diaz-Morales and Sorroche (2008); Prieto, Diaz-Morales and Barreno (2012)** suggested that the boys showed more morningness preference than the girls.

Table No. -5.24

Average academic performance scores of the subjects of four subgroups formed on the basis of personality (Agreeableness) and M-E preference

Personality (Agreeableness)	M-E preference		
	Morning type	Intermediate type	Evening type
High	M = 73.34 SD = 9.948 n = 163	M = 72.23 SD = 9.347 n = 122	M = 71.04 SD = 8.505 n =49
Low	M = 72.54 SD = 10.770 n = 116	M = 71.08 SD = 8.825 n = 144	M = 68.10 SD = 9.81 n = 58

The first-order interaction between personality and morningness-eveningness preference was also studied. The average academic performance scores of four subgroups formed on the basis of personality and morningness-eveningness preference are shown in table-5.24. Result of the ANOVA in table-5.21 findings indicated that the interaction between personality and morningness-eveningness preference was not significant F (2,671) = 1.101 = .333 (table-5.21). This insignificant interaction suggested that the academic performance scores of students of the high and low agreeable do not depend on morningness-eveningness preference.

Table No. -5.25

Average academic performance scores of the subjects of twelve subgroups formed on the basis of personality (Agreeableness), gender and morningnes-eveningness preference

Personality	**Gender**					
	Male Preference			**Female Preference**		
(Agreeableness)	**Morning Type**	**Intermediate Type**	**Evening Type**	**Morning Type**	**Intermediate Type**	**Evening Type**
High	M = 66.18 SD = 10.240 n = 61	M = 68.15 SD = 8.982 n = 66	M = 65.60 SD = 10.839 n = 30	M = 71.23 SD = 9.643 n = 61	M = 72.10 SD = 8.933 n = 62	M = 70.36 SD = 9.304 n = 25
Low	M = 69.44 SD = 9.623 n = 84	M = 68.05 SD = 10.004 n = 77	M = 68.33 SD = 9.927 n = 39	M = 81.57 SD = 6.344 n = 53	M = 77.08 SD = 7.441 n = 49	M = 72.31 SD = 6.237 n = 13

The second-order interaction gives a joint effect of personality, gender and morningness-eveningness preference. The average academic performance scores of the students of twelve subgroups were formed on the basis of personality (high and low), gender (male and female) and morningness-eveningness preference (morning type, intermediate type and evening type) shown in the table-5.25. The obtained F-ratio was not significant F (2, 671) = .355 = .701(table-5.21). This insignificant interaction concluded that the difference in academic performance exhibited by the students of low and high personality does not differ significantly because of different level of gender and morningness-eveningness preference.

Therefore, the above discussion makes it understandable that all the two factors i.e., personality and morningness-eveningness preference affect the academic performance independently but the personality does not influence the academic performance. The interaction between gender and morningness-eveningness preference jointly influence the academic performance of the students. However, the interaction between gender and personality and morningness-eveningness preference do not jointly affect the academic performance of the students' yet the second order interaction is found to be significant at any level.

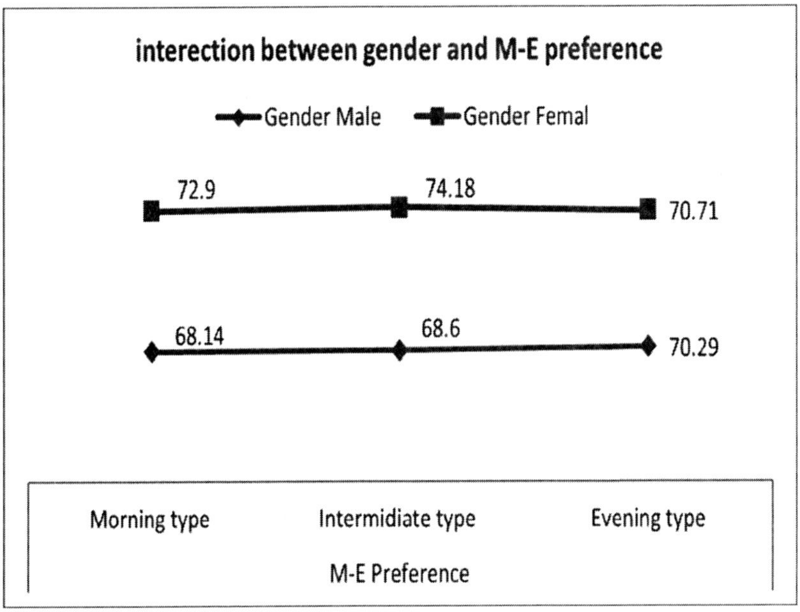

Figure- 16: Average academic performance scores of four subgroups formed on the basis of gender and morningness-eveningness preference

Personality Factor Conscientiousness

Table No. -5.26

Average academic performance scores of the groups of personality (Conscientiousness), gender and morningnes-eveningness preference

Variables	Groups	Average Scores of Academic Performance
Conscientiousness	High	71.18 n = 348
	Low	68.58 n = 238
Gender	Male	71.88 n =309
	Female	68.58 n = 277
Morningness-Eveningness Preference	Morning type	69.48 n = 248
	Intermediate type	71.23 n = 243
	Evening type	70.21 n = 95

The fifth problem of the present work was to examine whether the subjects showing low conscientiousness differ significantly in their academic performance than the subjects showing high conscientiousness. Those who score high on conscientiousness factor are efficient, organized, self disciplined orderly, dutiful, careful, competent, responsible and thorough full and those who score low on conscientiousness factor are careless, undependable, negligent, disorganized and irresponsible. Therefore, it was hypothesized that the subjects with low conscientiousness would show low academic performance than the subjects with high conscientiousness.

Table No. -5.27

Summary of three way analysis of variance for the data

Source	Sum of Square	df	Mean Square	F Ratio	Sig
Conscientious-ness	1233.861	1	1233.861	13.360	.000**
Gender	1767.557	1	1767.557	19.139	.000**
M-E Preference	844.686	2	422.343	4.573	.011**
Conscientious-ness * Gender	8.593	1	8.593	.093	.760
Gender* M-E Preference	257.576	2	128.788	1.395	.249
Conscientious-ness * M-E Pref-erence	1.283	2	.641	.007	.993
Conscientious-ness*Gender*M-E Preference	193.647	2	96.824	1.048	.351
Error	53010.493	574	92.353		
Total	**2957888.000**	**586**			

An observation of table-5.26, figure-17 findings indicated that the average academic performance scores of the students of high and low conscientiousness are 71.88 and 68.58 respectively, and the obtained F-ratio for the personality factor were found to be significant, $F(1, 574) = 13.360$, $p < .01$ level (table-5.27). The significant F-ratio indicated that the personality factor conscientiousness has a significant effect on academic performance of the students. It means the students who have high scores in conscientiousness show high academic performance as compared to those who have low scores in conscientiousness. Thus, the obtained results have confirmed the hypothesis. The possible reason of conscientious individuals showing better academic performance is due to the fact that the students who are honest, well-organized, careful, self disciplined, reliable and responsible show good academic outcomes. Conscientious students are more likely to work hard and complete their projects, coursework or assignments. Conscientiousness will be significantly related to performance. Therefore, it is expected that conscientious individuals will perform better in class, obtain better essay marks, and have lower levels of absence. The findings of this result supported the findings of the **Blickle (1996); Busato et al. (2000); De Raad and Schouwenburg (1996); Furnham and Chamorro-Premuzic (2003); Chowdhury (2006); Conard (2006); Komarraju, Karau, Ronald, Schmeck and Advic (2011); Kling (2001); Koning Loyens, Rikers, Smeets and Molen (2012); Laidra, Pullmann, and Allik (2007); McKenzie and Gow (2004); Rogers (2005); Salgado (1997); Wright (2008)** who had reported that conscientiousness is positively related to academic performance. Consequently, organised, careful, discipline, hardworking, persevering, and achievement-oriented students may be expected to be successful in academic settings **(Furnham et al., 2003; Moutafi, Furnham, & Crump, 2003). Nur Safwati, Nur Syaliza, Nur fatihah and Nur Dalila (2014)** reported that the conscientiousness dimension was a positive predictor of academic success.

Gender (male and female) was considered as the second independent variable. It was assumed that female would show higher academic performance than male. An observation of table-5.26, figure-18 findings indicated that the average academic performance scores of the male and female students are 67.91 and 73.84 respectively, and the obtained F-ratio for the gender was found to be significant at $F (1, 574) = 19.139$, $p < .01$ level (table 5.27). The significant F- ratio indicates that the gender significantly affects the academic performance of students. The female students show a higher academic performance as compared to male students. Therefore, the obtained results have confirmed the hypothesis that the female subjects would show a high academic performance than the male subjects. We have already seen in the previous part of the studies that the gender influences the academic performance i.e., **(Abubakar & Uboh, 2010; Allon-Lee & Paat, 2001; Amitava, Maojit, Saawata**

and Braja, 2010; Delgdo & Collado, 2011; Epstein, Elwood, Hey and Maw De, 1998; Escribano, Iaz-Morales, Fergusson & Horwood 1997; Hyde and Linn, 2006; Mirza & Malik, 2000; Mishra & Jha, 2014; Mullies, Martin, Gonzalez, & Kennedy, 2003; Rana, 2002; Spelke, 2005; Weaver-Hightower, 2003; Wong, Lam, and Ho, 2002) who observed that the female students perform better as compared to male students. However, the findings of the present study reveal that the female show higher academic performance than male.

Morningness-Eveningness Preference i.e., morning type, intermediate type and evening type was considered as the third independent variable. It was assumed that the subjects with morning preference would show a higher academic performance than the subjects with evening preference and subjects with intermediate preference would remain in between the above two. An observation of table-5.26, figure-19 findings indicated that the average academic performance scores of the morning type, intermediate type and evening type students are 69.48, 71.23 and 70.21 respectively, and the obtained F-ratio for the morningness-eveningness preference was found to be significant at $F(2, 574) = 4.573$, $p < .01$ level (table-5.27). A significant F-ratio indicated that the morningness-eveningness preference significantly influenced the academic performance of the students. The intermediate and evening type perform better as compared to morning type. Thus, the obtained results have not confirmed the hypothesis.

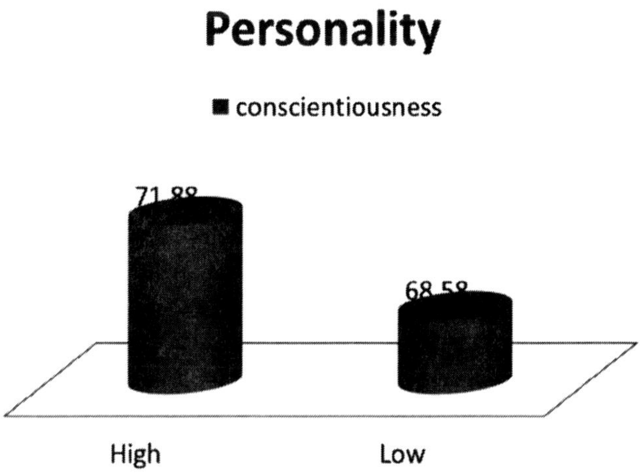

Figure- 17: (Personality) average academic performance scores of high and low conscientiousness

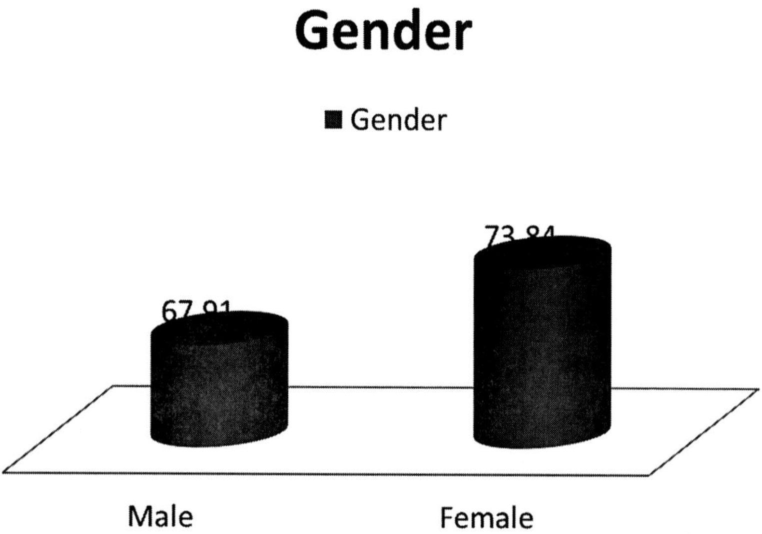

Figure- 18: (Gender) average academic performance scores of male and female

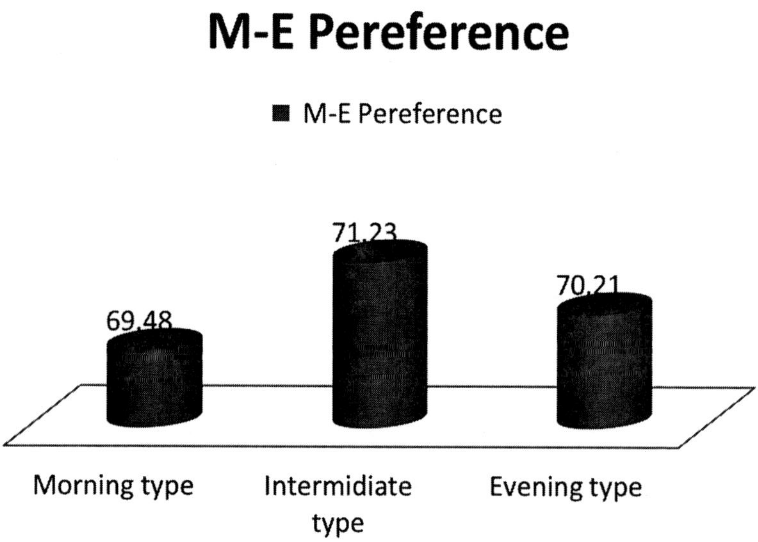

Figure – 19: (Morningness-Evenigness preference) average academic performance scores of morning active, intermediate active and evening active

So far, we have discussed the interaction between the independent variables i.e. personality (Conscientiousness), gender and morningness-eveningness preference.

Table No. -5.28

Average academic performance scores of the subjects of four subgroups formed on the basis of personality (Conscientiousness) and gender

Personality (Conscientiousness)	Gender	
	Male	Female
High	M = 69.22 SD = 10.074 n = 165	M = 74.92 SD = 8.637 n = 144
Low	M = 66.73 SD = 10.501 n = 183	M = 72.19 SD = 8.541 n = 94

The first order interaction is between personality (Conscientiousness) and gender. The average academic performance score of four subgroups formed on the basis of personality (conscientiousness) and gender are shown in table-5.28. Result of the ANOVA in table-5.27 findings indicated that the interaction between personality (conscientiousness) and gender was not found significant F (1, 574) = .093 =.760 (table-5.27). This insignificant interaction suggested that the academic performance of the students' high and low extravert do not depend on gender. It may be said that the insignificant F-ratio prove that both factors - personality and gender – are independent in exerting their influence on academic performance.

Table No. -5.29

Average academic performance scores of the subjects of four subgroups formed on the basis of gender and M-E preference

Gender	M-E preference		
	Morning type	**Intermediate type**	**Evening type**
Male	M = 67.37 SD = 11.175 n = 151	M = 68.14 SD = 808 n = 135	M = 68.73 SD = 9.530 n = 62
Female	M = 72.75 SD = 9.341 n = 97	M = 75.08 SD = 7.885 n = 108	M = 73.00 SD = 8.916 n = 33

The first-order interaction between gender and morningness-eveningness preference was also studied. The average academic performance scores of four subgroups formed on the basis of gender and morningness-eveningness preference are shown in table-5.29. Result of the ANOVA in table-5.27 findings indicated that the interaction between gender and morningness-eveningness preference was found to be not significant F (2, 574) = 1.395 = .249 (table-5.27). This insignificant interaction suggested that the academic performance scores of students of gender i.e., male and female are not dependent upon the morningness-eveningness preference i.e., morning type, intermediate type and evening type. It may be said that the academic performance scores of male and female students do not depend on the level of morningness-eveningness preference.

Table No. -5.30

Average academic performance scores of the subjects of four subgroups formed on the basis of personality (Conscientiousness) and M-E preference

Personality (Conscientiousness)	M-E preference		
	Morning type	**Intermediate type**	**Evening type**
High	M = 70.62 SD = 10.418 n = 177	M = 73.58 SD = 8.954 n = 110	M = 73.55 SD = 7.884 n = 22
Low	M = 66.63 SD = 11.282 n = 71	M = 69.28 SD = 9.763 n = 133	M = 69.21 SD = 9.757 n = 73

The first-order interaction between personality and morningness-eveningness preference was also studied. The average academic performance scores of four subgroups formed on the basis of personality and morningness-eveningness preference are shown in table-5.30. Result of the ANOVA in table-5.27 findings indicated that the interaction between personality and morningness-eveningness preference was found to be not significant F (2, 574) = .007 = .993 (table-5.27). This insignificant interaction suggested that the academic performance scores of students of the high and low conscientiousness do not depend on morningness-eveningness preference.

Table No. -5.31

Average academic performance scores of the subjects of twelve subgroups formed on the basis of personality (Conscientiousness), gender and morningnes-eveningness preference

Per-sonality (Conscientiousness)	Gender					
	Male Preference			Female Preference		
(Neuroticism)	Morning Type	Intermediate Type	Evening Type	Morning Type	Intermediate Type	Evening Type
High	M = 67.96 SD = 10.976 n = 95	M = 70.55 SD = 8.674 n = 56	M = 72.50 SD =7.753 n = 14	M = 73.70 SD = 8.841 n = 82	M = 76.72 SD = 8.190 n = 82	M = 75.38 SD = 8.297 n = 8
Low	M = 66.33 SD = 11.536 n = 56	M = 66.43 SD = 10.250 n = 79	M = 67.62 SD = 10.602 n = 48	M = 67.60 SD = 10.602 n = 15	M = 73.44 SD = 7.278 n = 54	M = 72.24 SD = 9.135 n = 25

The second-order interaction gives a joint effect of personality, gender and morningness-eveningness preference. The average academic performance scores of the students of twelve subgroups formed on the basis of personality (high and low), gender (male and female) and morningness-eveningness preference (morning type, intermediate type and evening type) are shown in table-5.31. The obtained F-ratio was not significant F (2, 574) = 1.048 = .351 (table-5.27). This insignificant interaction concluded that the difference in academic performance exhibited by the students of low and high personality does not differ significantly because of different level of gender and morningness-eveningness preference.

Therefore, the above discussion makes it understandable that all the three factors i.e., personality, gender and morningness-eveningness preference influence the academic performance independently. However, none of their interaction is found to be significant at any level.

CONCLUSION

The present research concluded that the personality factor i.e., neuroticism, gender and morningness-evesningness preference affect the academic performance independently; there was a significant interaction between gender and neuroticism and between morningness-eveningness preference and neuroticism except interaction between gender and morningness-eveningness preference. The second order interaction was not found significant.

1. Personality factor, i.e., extraversion and gender affect the academic performance independently but there was no significant effect of morningness-eveningness preference. However, none of their interaction was found significant.

2. Personality factor, i.e., openness, gender and morningness-eveningness preference affect the academic performance independently, gender and morningness-eveningness preference and morningness-eveningness preference and openness jointly did not affect the academic performance but gender and openness jointly did not influence the academic performance. The second-order interaction was found not significant.

3. Personality factor, i.e., agreeableness did not significantly influence the academic performance, but gender and morningness-eveningness preference affected the academic performance independently. The joint effect of gender and morningness-eveningness preference was found significant but the joint effect of gender and agreeableness and morningness-eveningness preference and agreeableness was not significant, yet the second order interaction was not found significant.

4. Personality factor i.e., conscientiousness, gender and morningness-eveningness preference influenced the academic performance independently, but none of the interaction was found significant.

*****